To John
From Mary. Happy Birthday

Pub
SPEED MAP — 41 (T151)
LANCASHIRE
MAP + FIELD NAMES 162

(wonderful stonework)

John Bentley

PORTRAIT OF WYCOLLER

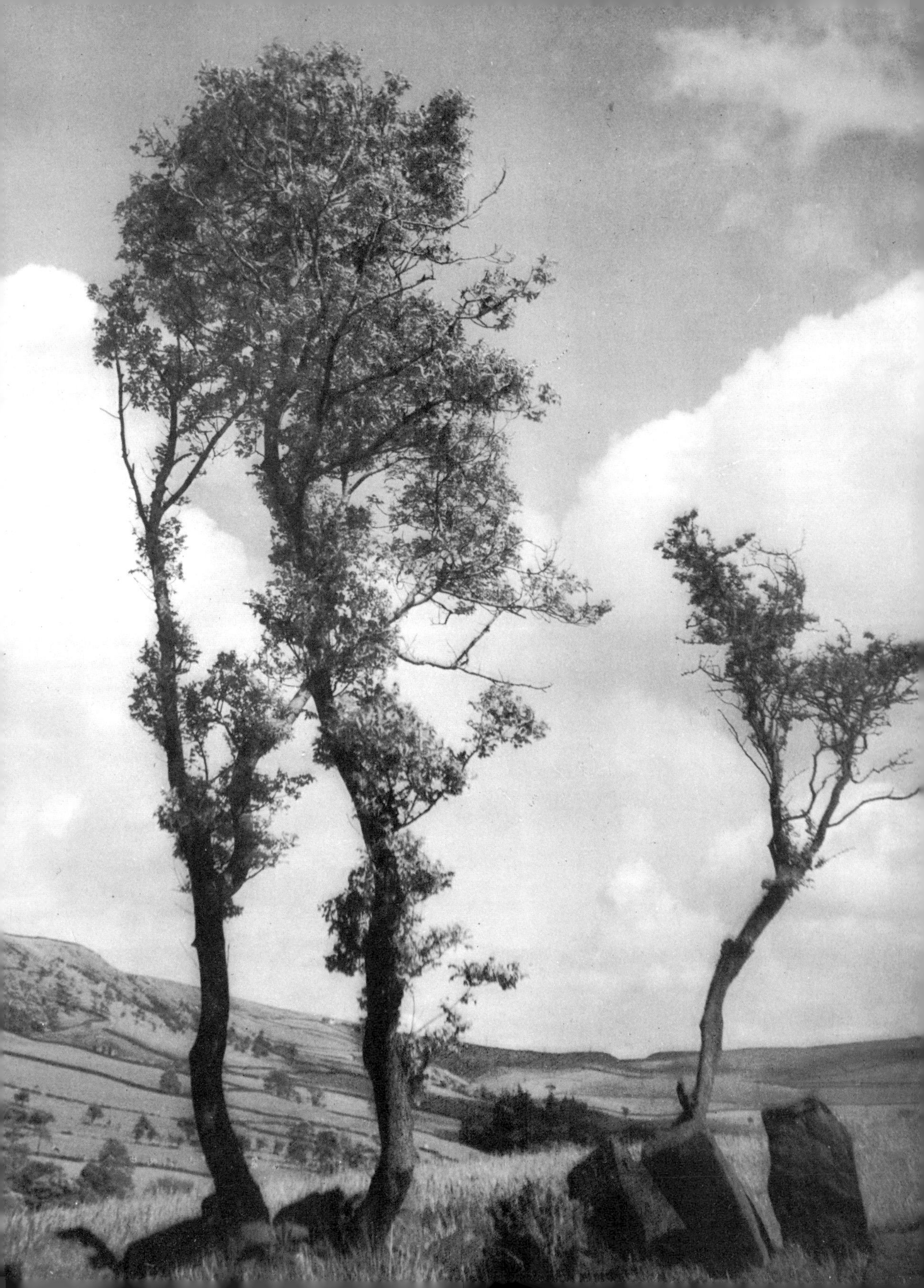

PORTRAIT OF WYCOLLER

BY JOHN BENTLEY

NELSON LOCAL HISTORY SOCIETY, 1975

ISBN 0 9502614 3 2

Printed by Fretwell & Brian Ltd., Silsden, Keighley, West Yorkshire.

Contents

	Acknowledgements	
	Introduction	
1.	Arrow-heads and Axes	9
2.	Vaccaries in the Forest	18
3.	Tudor Times	30
4.	Stuart Period	48
5.	Thomas Eyre's Account	63
6.	The Last Squire	73
7.	Ghosts and Legends	88
8.	Wycoller in Literature	102
9.	People and Work	130
10.	Farms, Fields and Cottages	139
11.	Valley of the Seven Bridges	167
12.	Saved from the Flood	177
13.	Friends and Preservation	184
14.	Country Park	196
	Sources and Notes	200
	Bibliography	204
	Index	205

Acknowledgements

The author wishes to thank Peter Facer, M.A., for his assistance in preparing this book for printing. Thanks are also due to R. Sharpe France, M.A., the Lancashire County Archivist for the transcription of documents; to Wilfred M. Spencer, F.L.A., for the loan of deeds, documents and maps; to Allan Dalby, Gladys Whittaker and Doreen Crowther for transcripts of documents and registers relating to Wycoller; to Richard Hartley of Bridge End Farm, Rimington for the loan of deeds; to Douglas Barber, B.A., for the loan of the correspondence of Wycoller Preservation Committee; to Ralph C. Cross for information and suggestions; to Stanley Cookson for the loan of maps and documents and to Nesta Wood for permission to reproduce her poetry.

The author is indebted to the Lancashire Record Office for the assistance of staff and permission to reproduce documents; to the Brontë Society for access to books; to Peter Wightman and the staff at Colne Library for ready access to all their material concerning Wycoller and to Susan Hunt, reference librarian at Nelson Library for assistance.

Photographs and Illustrations

The new photographic work for this book has been undertaken by Arthur Charlesworth of Barrowford and the admirable results can be seen on pages 9, 10, 24, 36, 85, 96, 106, 139, 140, 141, 142, 143, 144, 145, 146, 148, 149, 155, 156, 170, 175, 198.
The majority of other photographs have come from the collection of Charles Green of Foulridge. Further photographs were loaned by Colne Library, Stanley Cookson, Frank and Nesta Dewhurst, Maggie Bracewell, Wilfred M. Spencer, F.L.A., Clifford Byrne and Roland and Mary Walton. Drawings and the map of Wycoller's bridges were prepared by Carol Y. Bentley.

Introduction

It is now a quarter of a century since the publication of *Romantic Wycoller* by E. W. Folley. The only other publication specifically concerned with Wycoller and the Cunliffe family was *The Descendants of the Elder Branch of the Cunliffes of Wycoller*, which was written and published by General C. H. Owen, R.A., in 1887.

In the last twenty five years many new sources of information have come to light and, as former publications are long out of print and almost impossible to obtain, it seemed to be worth taking a new look at this fascinating village. As material was being gathered together news came of Wycoller's salvation in the form of a Country Park and Conservation Area. This new development made it an ideal time for a new publication.

No previous writing on Wycoller has been uncritically accepted and where possible research has been done from original sources. Unpublished diaries, newly-discovered documents, recent archaeological discoveries, as well as routine research have added new and striking facts about Wycoller. Speaking of facts, J. J. Bagley's advice to the historian has been strictly adhered to, "He must revere the sacredness of facts—once he is satisfied that they are indeed facts. Theories and interpretations of the past, however hallowed or long-standing, always remain mortal and expendable. Facts stand unmovable".

Although many errors found in past writings have been corrected and a great deal of new information added, this book does not profess to be the last word on Wycoller, but rather another stage in the revelation of its story. In years to come further research and archaeological evidence will surely reveal more.

Defending historians against the general belief that they are concerned only with dead and dusty records, G. M. Trevelyan explained, "But to us, as we read, they take form, colour, gesture, passion, thought. It is only by study that we can see our forerunners, remote and recent, in their habits as they lived, intent each on the business of a long-vanished day, riding out to do homage or to poll a vote; to seize a neighbour's manor-house and carry off his ward, or to leave cards on ladies in crinolines". This book is, therefore, an attempt to present the panorama of Wycoller from prehistoric times to the present day so that it may take form and colour for you and bring to life the many fascinating aspects of its past.

John Bentley.

Arrow-heads and Axes

Beneath the peat on the moors overlooking Wycoller lie flints left by the people who came to live there after the retreat of the glaciers some twelve thousand years ago. These men of the Mesolithic or Middle Stone Age lived and hunted on these moors and left evidence of their occupation. The evidence is in the form of small sharp flints, known as pygmy flints because of their small size. These small flint blades were mainly used as barbs set in hunting weapons made of wood or bone. Many are well shaped and finely worked while others appear merely as flint chippings. These flints are common to all the moorland areas of the Pennines. Flint is luckily little affected by the passing of time, but all other evidence of these early settlers has either been destroyed by the acid peat soil or at least covered by it.

Since late prehistoric times our local moors have been slowly blanketed by a thick layer of peat. This peat growth, caused by the slow decomposition of organic matter in moorland areas as the climate became colder and wetter, has spread and deepened over wide areas. Where the peat is eroded by wind and rain flints are often washed out.

Also beneath the peat on the summit and slopes of Boulsworth lie the remains of prehistoric forests, some remains are as deep as three metres below the present ground level. Here can be found trunks, branches, twigs, roots and bark from the trees that grew in the periods following the last ice age. Early man would hunt a great variety of animals in these woods, including foxes, wolves, deer, boar and aurochs, the ancestor of domestic cattle.

Neolithic settlers

Some six thousand years ago Neolithic people entered the area. These Neolithic settlers from the continent were involved in agriculture well before 3,000 B.C. and they too left evidence of their

Wood, twigs and bark—the remains of prehistoric woodland from the peat on the slopes of Boulsworth Hill

settlement. Although they lived on the higher ground these early settlers came down into the Wycoller valley and left evidence of their presence. In September 1957, Charles Green, a keen local historian, found a prehistoric hammer-stone half buried in clay near the road mid-way between Parson Lee Farm and Parson Lee Out Laithe. This stone of reddish quartzite is an excellent example of a prehistoric hammer-stone. The compact weight of quartz made it a useful material for such implements which would be used to shape flints. The wear on this stone suggests that it has also been used for polishing small objects, such as knives of flint. The hammer-stone is still in the possession of Charles Green and may eventually be left to the Country Park at Wycoller.

When Charles Green first found this stone he thought that he had found a rubbing stone used for grinding corn in a saddle quern, especially as he knew that not long before a saddle quern had been found on Combe Hill overlooking Wycoller. This saddle quern was discovered in October 1955 by Joe Davies a local archaeologist. The Neolithic farmers ground their corn on a wide and shallow

Saddle quern

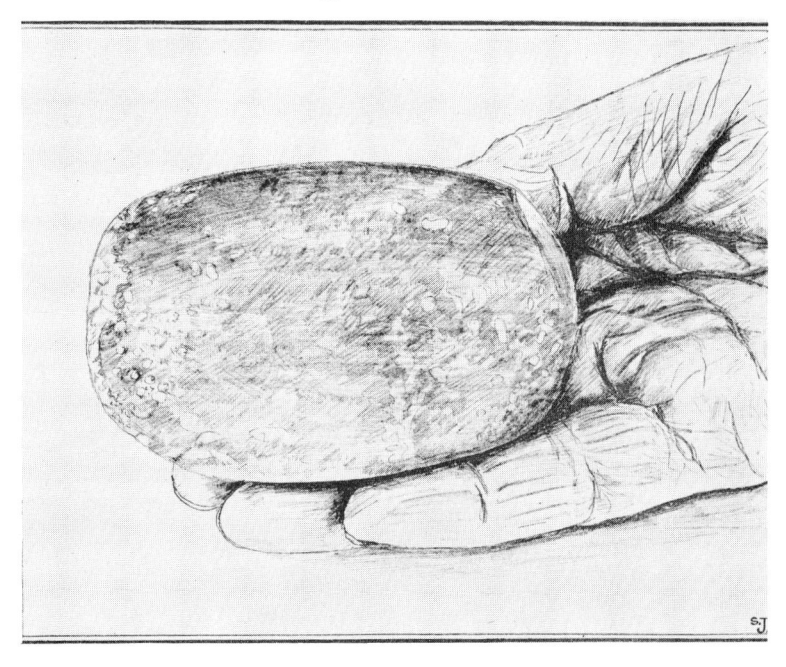

Quartzite hammer-stone from Parson Lee

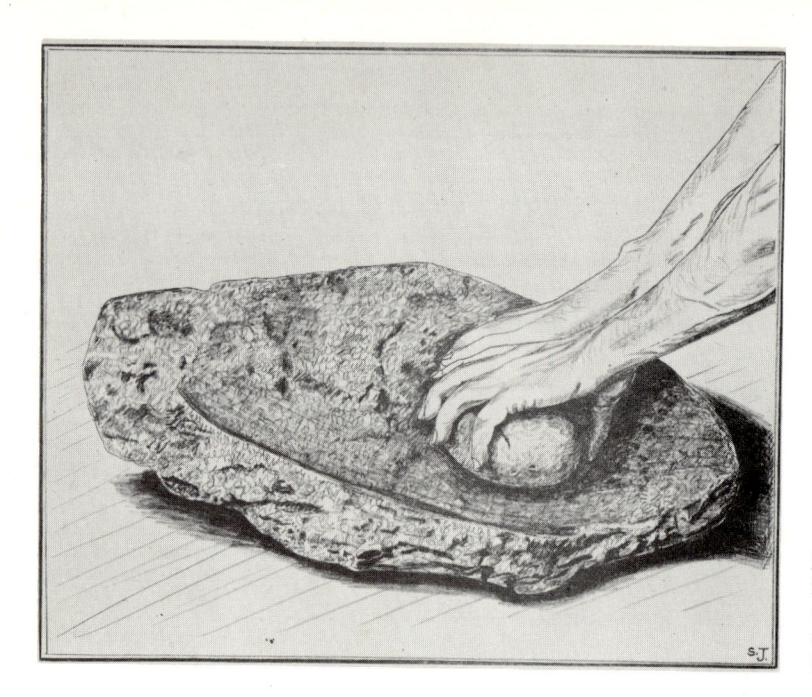

Saddle quern found lying face upward on the eroded peat at Combe Hill

stone basin using a rubbing stone which they ground round and round using one hand. These saucer querns gradually developed into saddle querns in which the large upper stone, which could be held in two hands, was rubbed on a lower stone with a forward and backward motion. Through continued wear the stone often became saddle shaped.

Saddle querns were in use from Neolithic or Early Bronze Age times down to the early Iron Age when they were superseded by the more efficient rotary querns, known as beehive querns. This saddle quern is the only one of its type found in the area and is 55 centimetres long and 35 centimetres at its widest part. It is 14 centimetres thick at the top and tapers to 4 centimetres at the bottom. It is made of local gritstone and shows worn down quartz pebbles in its surface. The hollowed area is 35 centimetres by 25 centimetres and is about 5 centimetres deep in the centre. Joe Davies commented that, "it may be inferred that a considerable amount of grit went into prehistoric bread, with disastrous effect on prehistoric teeth". Here is local evidence, in local material, of settled agriculture.

The Neolithic people were the first farmers of plants and animals and this change laid down the foundations of the civilisation which followed. We are so used to thinking of Neolithic as a period of set time in relation to our country that we forget that this period differs from country to country and area to area. 'Neolithic' simply implies food production based on the growing of crops and the rearing of animals, without the use of metals. Hunting continued alongside Neolithic agriculture, as farming was still hazardous and unreliable.

It was the Neolithic people who began to clear the forests that had spread over the higher land after the end of glacial times. They tackled the forests by burning and clearing, and their polished stone axes have been found in the area. One found recently within the boundaries of Wycoller lay in a stream bed under a culvert on the Laneshawbridge to Haworth road. Modern experiments with genuine Neolithic axes have shown that six hundred square metres of silver birch can be cleared in four hours and that a hundred trees can be felled with a stone axe not sharpened for four thousand years.

Perhaps Flint Age would have been a more suitable name for a prehistoric era than Stone Age, for flint has a quality far above that ever suggested by the mundane 'stone'. Flint was so suitable for prehistoric man to work and with it he was able to fashion the most effective and useful tools. The material is also attractive with its smooth glasslike quality and a well-fashioned arrow-head is a delight to examine with its finely shaped surface, razor edge and needle point.

Flint implements

Flint is luckily foreign to the area and so the majority of finds can be safely connected to prehistoric man. In Neolithic and Bronze Age times flints were developed into a wide range of instruments providing not just arrow-heads and knives, but borers, scrapers, gouges, saws, drills and chisels. The craft of flint work was raised into an industry and what has been termed a 'flint workshop' was discovered near Wycoller in 1899. The discoverer, Peter Whalley, was a keen local archaeologist and he spent some time making a thorough investigation of the area. The site on the slopes of Boulsworth near the ruins of Robin Hood's House was discovered where shooting boxes had been built and the ground disturbed leaving flints on the surface. The discovery of such a rich mine of prehistoric relics on the borders of Wycoller has a strong bearing on its history.

Flint knapper
at work

Peter Whalley found a large collection of flint scrapers, varying in length from two to six centimetres. He also found a valuable collection of flint arrow-heads of every conceivable variety, including heart-shaped, triangular and notched. There was a splendid collection of flint wedges and hundreds of small chippings. A heavy piece of red porphyry found on the site was taken to be a flint knapping stone. After the death of Peter Whalley part of this collection was left to Colne Library.

In 1965, although known to many local historians, the site was re-discovered, without realising that others had been there before, by Harry Stansfield, a keen moor walker and student of prehistoric settlement. Removing a large amount of peat he discovered thousands of flints, several hammer stones and a large anvil stone around which there were hundreds of flint chippings. This collection includes both hunting and domestic tools. The lack of potsherds, jewellery and other artefacts, and the style of flints suggests that this site was occupied for some thousands of years between 10,000 B.C. and 3,000 B.C. After 3,000 B.C. tanged and barbed arrow-heads, spindle whorls and other domestic objects might be expected.

(Above) Flint thumb scraper from Wycoller

(Left) Tanged and barbed flint arrow-head of the Bronze Age

The site on the rise of a hill presented a different world to these early settlers. The ground was rich with grass and birch woods and, of course, the climate was very much warmer. Today with the growth of a considerable depth of black peat and the deterioration of the weather, the moors present a bleak picture for much of the year.

Although no bronze implements of the Bronze Age have been found in Wycoller, they have been found on the moors not many miles away. However, many Bronze Age flints have been found in the area, and the most attractive one is a tanged and barbed arrow-head found by Stanley Cookson on Combe Hill in 1969. This finely-worked flint is almost transparent and when found was still needle sharp.

A suspected Bronze Age burial mound at Brink Ends in Wycoller was excavated by Stanley Cookson in 1971 and 1972. Although no interment was discovered the remains of a fire was found in the centre of the mound with half burnt twigs and coal. Some small cubes of coal stood on a fire-burnt stone yet the coal had only just begun to ignite.

Bronze Age burial

Cairn said to be a Middle Bronze Age burial

Boulder stone walls on the south side of Wycoller Beck suggest an Iron Age settlement and the occurrence of a clam bridge, the earliest and most primitive bridge in Wycoller, supports the theory. Stanley Cookson has strong suspicions that an Iron Age settlement existed in this area but only time and further exploration will tell.

Although nothing of Roman origin has been found in the valley it must be remembered that Wycoller is not very far from Ribchester, Roman Bremetennacum, near to Elslack and close to a Roman road. Ribchester was garrisoned by cavalry with a duty to protect the roads in the area from both the wild tribes of the surrounding countryside and from the raids of Irish pirates, who could sail their boats up the lower waters of the Ribble.

The local people were known to the Romans as Brigantes. We know little about them but their fate under the Romans is quite clear. At first a client-state they later rebelled against the Romans on several occasions. They were defeated, their lands ravaged, their forts slighted and many of their leaders captured and executed. It is likely that the local Roman roads would be built by Brigantes in conscripted labour gangs. The close proximity of Roman cavalry at Ribchester makes it possible that they visited the Wycoller valley. Cavalry exercises, as well as intelligence work would take them to most local settlements. Effort would be made to keep in touch with village chiefs and keep a finger on the pulse of the civilian population. There was also the question of trade, the Romans needed many items from the native British including cloth, hides and food. There is, however, no definite evidence of Roman activity in the Wycoller area.

Most writers have tended to underestimate the existence of prehistoric man in the area. Walter Bennett in *The History of Marsden and Nelson* says that "neither huts nor camping sites have ever been found to show that Neolithic man settled for any length of time in this district though many flint instruments found on the neighbouring moors show that they hunted here". Others have also put forward this theory that early people only came into the area for hunting. However, the evidence of a well-worn saddle quern, thousands of flint instruments and other material suggests that permanent settlements were more likely to have been the case. Looking at the situation nationally there are few proven prehistoric domestic sites in any part of the country—huts of mud and branches simply do not survive over thousands of years especially in moorland areas.

This was explained clearly in *Field Archaeology* by the Ordnance Survey: "In the last two thousand years peat has blanketed most of our moorlands with a steady growth which has abolished woodland from all higher grounds and buried not only the camping sites of the Mesolithic hunters, but also hut sites, stone-walled enclosures, ancient fields, stone clearance heaps, burial mounds . . . and many other relics of life on the uplands before the onset of less favourable weather in the early part of the first Millenium B.C.". It is fairly certain that all the above mentioned types of prehistoric remains lie under the peat on the Wycoller moors—the task of discovery would be colossal. It should be quite safe to say that Wycoller and the moors that surround it have seen the comings and goings of man for some ten thousand years and continuous occupation during the last three thousand.

A view once to be seen in the Wycoller valley

Vaccaries in the Forest

Deer once drank at Wycoller Beck and roamed free both in the valley and on the moors, for Wycoller lay in the Forest of Trawden. A "forest" was then not necessarily all woodland. The Latin meaning of "foris" is "outside" and the word "forest" was applied to these large tracts of land because they were outside the ordinary law. Naturally, as these tracts of land were reserves for the king's beasts, they contained a large amount of woodland, and eventually the word "forest" became synonymous with woodland.

The Royal Forest

Whether Trawden Forest was set aside by the Saxon King Cnut or by the Normans is not clear, but it is likely that in the early days it was Royal Forest where beast counted over man and the harsh forest laws were enforced. Blinding, castration, the loss of hands and death were the punishments for interfering with the king's beasts. Moreover, the penalties could not only differ from crime to crime but from person to person. For the killing of a deer, for example, a freeman would be fined a large sum, for a serf the penalty was death.

The Royal Forest, the animals in it and the laws governing it are the subject of various and fascinating accounts. Richard fitz Nigel, treasurer to Henry II, gave his account in the *Dialogus*. The forests he said, "are the secret places of the kings and their great delight. To them they go for hunting, having put off their cares, so that they may enjoy a little quiet. There, away from the continuous business and incessant turmoil of the court, they can for a little time breathe in the grace of natural liberty, wherefore it is that those who commit offences there lie under the royal displeasure alone".

In the reign of Elizabeth I, John Manwood wrote a treatise on the forest and forest laws but by then the subject was already history. According to Manwood, the forester could take a man if he was found at "dog-draw", "stable-stand", "back-bear", or "bloody-hand". Dog-draw defined the situation where a hunter was found with a dog in pursuit of a wounded deer. Stable-stand applied where a hunter was found in a position ready to fire at the deer with his bow. Back-bear was the term used where a deer had been killed and the guilty person was discovered in the act of carrying it away. Bloody-hand applied where a person was found in the forest with blood on his hands or clothes and thus under suspicion of having killed a deer.

Spaniels and greyhounds were forbidden in the forest but the mastiff was allowed provided that the claws and pelote of its forefeet were cut off to prevent it from attacking the deer. This cutting of the claws was termed "lawing" or "hambling". The foot of the animal was placed on a block of wood and then a chisel was used to strike off the claws by the skin at one blow. The Rev. T. D. Whitaker says that in Bowland the treatment depended not on the species but on the size of the dog. An iron ring was kept as a gauge, if the animal's foot could pass through the gauge then it escaped the operation.

Trawden Forest was included in the lands given to Roger de Poitou by William the Conqueror shortly after the conquest. Roger de Poitou granted the area to Robert son of Ilbert de Lacy of Pontefract, and the de Lacy family held the forest until the death of Henry de Lacy in 1311. At this time Trawden Forest passed into the hands of Thomas Earl of Lancaster who had married Alice, daughter of Henry de Lacy. On the execution of the Earl of Lancaster for treason in 1322 Trawden Forest reverted to Edward II and on his death in 1327 it was included in lands given to the Queen Dowager, Isabella, for the term of her life. The lands were later attached to the Duchy of Lancaster and so returned to the Crown. Trawden Forest was held by the Crown from the fourteenth century until 1661, when Charles II granted the Honor of Clitheroe and the Hundred of Blackburn to General George Monck, Duke of Albemarle.

Throughout the centuries the name Trawden Forest remained but the territory was frequently referred to as "the Forest or Chase of Trawden". Moor drivers were employed to keep the deer within the chase but there is little mention of deer after 1500. In Trawden Forest few felt guilty of poaching the deer, and when the risk was least the deer were taken. From time to time poaching became wholesale and it was necessary for a general warning to be issued. In 1411 the Sheriff of Lancaster was ordered to make a public proclamation at the next sessions in Lancaster against the hunting and killing of deer in the King's Forests of Bowland, Pendle, Rossendale and Trawden.

Living in the forest had its consolations for the inhabitants. There was dead wood for kindling and live wood for building. The inhabitants were allowed to dig free turf although they were fined for burning more than one fire. Other benefits could be gained at risk—acorns for pigs, extra wood, honey and bee swarms, a rabbit for the pot, and even occasional venison found its way to the peasant's table.

> *Besides in all this Isle there no such cattell be,*
> *For largenesee, Horne and Haire as those of Lancashire,*
> *So that from every part of England farre and neere,*
> *Men haunt her Marts fore store, as from her Race to breed.*
> *Michael Drayton.*

Wycoller vaccaries   As early as written records go there were cattle rearing farms in Wycoller. These farms were known as vaccaries, and at Wycoller there were two of them: one at Nether-Wycoller and the other higher in the valley at Over-Wycoller. These cattle farms were generally situated on the best grazing land in the river valleys and close to vast stretches of moorland suitable for summer grazing.

The cattle from the Wycoller vaccaries were taken onto Combe Hill and the slopes of Boulsworth for summer pasture. The Lancashire vaccaries may have been in existence at the time of the Norman Conquest, but the earliest mention is in the Pipe Roll dated Michaelmas 1196: "Purchase of stock and implements for the Royal demesnes depleted during Count John's rebellion in 1194. 445 head of stock, including bulls, cows, mares and ewes for the re-stocking of the vaccaries within the forests of Lancashire".

Exactly when the Wycoller vaccaries were established is a difficult and obscure problem. They probably developed over many generations and could easily have been in operation when the Romans established themselves in this country in the first century A.D. The Romans noted that the British possessed a large number of cattle and that they lived upon the flesh and milk of the animals. It has been suggested that the vaccaries were established to provide oxen, the main beast of burden at the time. In theory eight oxen were needed for each village plough and the vaccaries would provide these. Although an important element, cattle were also kept for food and milk, and food production was the basis of vaccary development.

From the twelfth century until the early sixteenth century there were five vaccaries in the Forest of Trawden. Two were at Beardshaw, one at Winewall and the remaining two at Wycoller. Vaccary farming was common to the other forests in Pendle and Rossendale, all of which came under the Honor of Clitheroe. The De Lacy accounts give a full survey of the cattle in the vaccaries for the years 1295 and 1305. Details of the stock of the Trawden Forest vaccaries are given under the names of the keeper but the exact locations are not recorded. However, Henry de Emmott was most probably the cow-keeper at Nether-Wycoller, as Emmott, his home, was close by. There is no proof of this but the lists of cattle in the five vaccaries are very much alike.

TROCHDENE

The Instaurator of Blackburnschyre, Robert de Heppehale, and the Instaurators and cowkeepers render their compotus at Ictenhille, 26 Jan. 1297, from 30 Sept. 1295 to 29 Sept. 1296.

Henry de Emot in the place of Adam son of Maulke renders his compotus of 40 cows and 1 bull of the remainder, and 6 of addition; total of 46 cows, 1 bull. Of which he counts 1 in murrain, hide and flesh 2s; 2 delivered to Simon le Geldehirde, and 4 to the Instaurator. 39 cows, 1 bull remain. Also 4 oxen of addition, delivered to G. the parker. Also 14 yearlings of the remainder: 5 steers and 9 heifers remain. Also 26 calves of the year: of which 6 in murrain, hides and flesh 6½d; 1 delivered to Simon le Geldehirde, and 4 to the Instaurator: 15 calves remain.

Total of cattle remaining in the vaccary: 39 cows, 1 bull, 5 steers, 9 heifers, 8 yearlings, 4 young heifers, and 15 calves.

The cattle in the other vaccaries in Trawden are listed in a similar manner, and there are cases of both calves and yearlings being "strangled by the wolf". The records show that men were paid to guard the calves from attack by wolves, which at this time were still prowling around Trawden Forest. The wolves were finally cleared from the Wycoller area in the mid-fourteenth century but only after the ruthless hunting of several centuries.

The vaccaries were supervised by the steward of the Honor of Clitheroe. Under the steward was a chief instaurator who was responsible for all the vaccaries in Blackburnshire and under him were sub-instaurators each responsible for one of the forests. Cow-keepers were responsible for the day-to-day running of the farms although they were under the control and regular inspection of the sub-instaurator. The keeper received the "white" or "lactage" which was, of course, the milk; butter and cheese would also be made. The cow-keeper in Wycoller would have the help of hired herdsmen to deal with the cattle. These herdsmen lived in the vicinity of the vaccary and their rough cottages would be the early development of the hamlet of Wycoller.

The cattle in the vaccaries would be a hardy breed, long in horn and thick in hide to withstand the rigours of the weather and the attack of wolves. The cattle were probably the descendants of Bos Longifrons, the cattle of the Roman period and earlier. Skulls of this type of cattle have been found in England with flints embedded in their skulls, which suggests their existence even in prehistoric times.

Before the advent of modern farming and the development of the turnip it is commonly believed that the majority of cattle were killed in the autumn and the meat salted and stored for the winter. This was supposed to be due to the lack of winter feed. However, the De Lacy accounts of cattle in the thirteenth and fourteenth centuries show no signs of this. Records appear to show that sufficient hay was provided for winter feed, cowsheds were built and certain sheltered fields were used as all-year pasture. There was all-year pasture in a field at Wycoller called Stirpenden, which lay above the water meetings in Wycoller Dene. The situation suggests that this long-held belief did not apply at Wycoller.

The cattle lists frequently show losses through murrain. As no other cattle disease is mentioned, various diseases may have been included in this term. From the cattle lists it appears to have been an endemic disease, recurring year by year and taking a regular percentage of cattle and horses. Of fifty two mares accounted for at Ightenhill in Burnley during 1295 nine died of the murrain. This cattle plague, said to have its origins in the east, appeared in this country in 1316 with terrible results. It frequently raged among the cattle of this area and in 1324 the vaccary at Merkelesdene was empty due to the murrain, and no one was willing to continue farming there. The disease is reported to have been highly infectious as well as fatal. The symptoms were often reported as follows:- loss of appetite among the animals, body trembling, inflamed gums, dull discharging eyes and severe diarrhoea—death followed within eight days. The most unpleasant feature was the fact that when beasts were reported dead of murrain there was always a price given for the sale of flesh and hide, the former most likely went as tainted meat into someone's cooking pot.

Murrain

As well as cattle pestilence those early days saw disastrous human pestilence, especially when the people's resistance was lowered by poor food. The Great Pestilence or Bubonic Plague originated in the east and was carried across Europe by the black rat. It came to England in 1348 and spread throughout England and Wales during 1349. This greatest plague epidemic of all time was reported to have killed over one third of the entire population.

An unusual feature of the vaccary areas in Trawden Forest is the large number of slab stone walls. These can be found in Wycoller, Winewall and the Beardshaw area of Trawden, in fact all the sites of the early forest vaccaries. Their existence at these sites and along the old trackways joining them is surely no coincidence and the term "vaccary walls" therefore seems most apt. The largest number of these walls are in Wycoller where the stones tend to be larger and more regular than those in the neighbouring vaccary areas. These stones are easiest seen at the top of the steps leading from the

Vaccary walls

The slab stones in this vaccary wall appear to have been split from thicker blocks, thus making matching pairs

end of Wycoller Hall to Tenter Field. They extend right to the Laneshawbridge-Haworth road, and travelling up that road towards the Herders they can be seen to the right of Height Laithe Farm, standing like rows of giant jagged teeth on the skyline.

Originally there must have been many more of these stones as many broken ones can be found in the dry stone walls along the Wycoller Winewall boundary. Others have been placed in the beck near the clam bridge in the Dene, and more have been used to cover small streams. Some walls shown in 1844 have since disappeared and some field shapes have changed. These unusual and fascinating rough-hewn stones present two main problems. Where were they quarried and when were they erected? The first question is not too difficult to answer as outcrop rock of similar type to the stones themselves is found along Combe Hill, with evidence of it having been quarried. The question of age poses a far greater problem as the walls have been attributed by some to the Romans by others to the Saxons, and the theory that they were erected in the Bronze Age has even been put forward. These walls bear no relation to the dry stone walls of the Pennines which are mostly of the eighteenth or nineteenth century. The vaccary walls are referred to in old deeds as "Ancient Inclosures". The walls split old fields such as Pepper Hill field and Hellman Heads and as these field names are likely to be Saxon at the earliest then the evidence is that the walls are much later. The most likely period for their erection was during the lordship of the De Lacys, especially around 1260 when they set up new vaccaries in Pendle Forest and re-organised others in the Honor. The available evidence suggests that these walls were constructed between the years 1100 and 1400.

In the summer of 1322 armed raiders rode into Wycoller, threatened the Herdsmen there and drove off the cattle from the vaccaries. The same raiders drove away cattle from the vaccaries in Pendle Forest and horses from the stud farm at Ightenhill. The same summer, on 17 June, Robert Bruce crossed the border with a Scottish army. Bypassing Carlisle he burnt Rose Castle and then plundered down through Furness to Cartmel. Crossing the sands the Scots finally stopped at Preston, but Lancashire as far as Chorley and Healey Park was ransacked. The Scots returned over the border after five weeks of plundering, cattle rustling and ravaging the north west.

Raids on the vaccaries

These troubles had begun after the execution of Thomas Earl of Lancaster at Pontefract on 22 March 1322, six days after the Battle of Boroughbridge. Lancaster, Henry De Lacy's son-in-law, had struggled with the King for some time. After the murder of Gaveston, the subject of the King's affection, however, the King ardently opposed the murderers. Thomas Earl of Lancaster was among those responsible. It was not surprising, in this situation, that Robert Bruce took the chance not only to establish himself more firmly in Scotland but also to plunder the north country at his pleasure. The Earl of Lancaster was supposed to be holding back the Scots but did little to stop their plundering. Eventually

Edward marched against Lancaster and defeated him at Boroughbridge in March 1322. The story is told that Lancaster sought refuge in the church and fell before the altar, from where he was dragged by his enemies. His execution in his own castle at Pontefract, facing Scotland, was a final humiliation.

Disturbances in the forest

Serious disturbances broke out in the north country territories which, previously owned by Lancaster, had now been seized by Edward. This land included the Forest of Trawden where stags were killed and cattle stolen. At the taking of a survey of the Manor of Colne on 3 October 1323 it was stated: "They also say that as to trespass of thieves in the forests and parks, and as to hunting, they are ignorant, and cannot say anything. They also say that a great multitude of animals viz., mares foals, bulls and cows—have been driven away from Hightinhill to Skipton by they know not whom, nor can they say anything as to the number or value". On the following day at an inquisition at the Manor of Ightenhill in Burnley the jury found "that Nicholas Mauleverer, then Constable of Skypton Castle, with many others from Cravin and Ayredale, did take from the horse rearing establishment at Ightenhill, and from the stock farms of Penhul and Troudene, various animals and did make waste of the King's wine at Ightinhill, to his loss, as they understand of ccxxxij.lib.vj.solid. (£232. 6s.)".

Edward II at Burnley

King Edward II himself was present at this inquisition at Burnley and stayed at Ightenhill Manor for several days in October 1323. That these troubles created a great deal of fear in the local inhabitants is shown by the jury who knew nothing of thieves, were ignorant of hunting, and had no idea who had driven off the cattle to Skipton. It is unlikely that anyone in the area was ignorant of what had gone on, let alone a picked jury of the leading inhabitants of the forest—they were just not saying.

In 1326 Queen Isabella, who had been in France, returned with an army and forced Edward to abdicate in favour of their son. Edward was imprisoned in Berkeley Castle and in September 1327 he was murdered with a red hot poker. After the disturbances of 1322 the King had not been keen to re-stock the vaccaries and risk further losses. The remaining animals seem to have been concentrated in Rossendale and Pendle Forests while the Wycoller vaccaries and others in Trawden Forest were rented out. In 1323 "Over Wycolure" vaccary was let at 14s. and "Nether Wycolure" at 16s. The accounts of 1324 to 1325 show that "Over Wycolure" was leased by John of the Ewode and "nether Wycolure" by Adam son of Henry. In 1341 the rents for each vaccary were 46s. 8d. but no leaseholders' names are given.

TROUDENE

The herbage of the vaccary of Wyculre to farm from S.S. Giles and Michael 46s. 8d.

The herbage of another vaccary there S.S. Giles and Michael 46s. 8d.

Under wages and expenditure the following points were noted:-

Building of folds at Wiculre and Berdshaghe for animals impounded in the chase of Troudene.

2s. 0d.

Wages of carpenter felling timber in wood and 4 parts of cruckes, railis, hergerell, lattis and other necessary timber for lengthening and repairing a shippon in Wynewall and for carpentry on the site by agreement 6s. 0d.

Carriage of timber	12d.
Iron nails	17½d.
Clearing the site	6d.
Mowing rushes for thatching	3s. 0d.
Building a house for the heifers there	2s. 6d.

The herdsmen and their families in Wycoller continued their routine lives, and the glimpses we get are from the few documents that by good fortune have survived the centuries. The compotus of John de Cronkshagh and John Clerk, "collector of the herbage for Blackburnshir," from Michaelmas 1422 to Michaelmas 1423 include these most interesting accounts for Trawden.

And for trespass of beasts in the Forest there called winter agistment, nothing, because in the chase the grass is consumed by the King's animals.

And for summer herbage, nothing, for the same reason. And for grass sold for mowing nothing, because it is reserved for the King's wild animals.

And for escape of beasts, nothing, because it is reserved to the farmer of the vaccary in his demise or lease.

And for 113s. 4d. received from Geoffrey de Hertley and Robert de Hertley, for farm of the grass of Over-wycolur and Nether-wycolur vaccaries, demised to them by the Steward for 10 years, this fifth year. The old rent was £4. 10s. 0d. equally in two titles.

Perhaps some of the above comments were a hint to the King that it would be to his financial benefit to curtail the activities of the deer and allow the development of farming. The nil returns continue in other accounts and are most humorous in the accounts of Sir John Stanley, Master Forester of the Forests of Blackburnshire. His return for the year Michaelmas 1434 to Michaelmas 1435 contains the following items:

> *And for nothing for the escape of beasts from the launds in Penhull and Trovedene, because none happened.*
> *And for nothing from Turbary at Riggende, in Penhull, because it is James Bannister's farm.*
> *And for nothing from croppings of branches, loppings, bark of oaks, either felled for the repair of pales of the parks or thrown down by the wind, in Penhull, Rossendale, or Troveden, this year.*
> *And for nothing from honey or wax, as there happened to be none that year.*
> *And for nothing from any profit arising from suit of gaol or estrays.*

This is one way of making a list much longer and more impressive but it did not increase the accounts. Accounts such as this would certainly be investigated by taxation authorities today—perhaps they were questioned then!

Few of the names of the inhabitants of mediaeval Wycoller have survived. In 1443, however, the first full list of the tenants and freeholders is included under Trawden in a list covering the Honor of Clitheroe.

TRAWDEN A.D. 1443.

John Clerk, for Edmund Parker
Laurence Parker, for le Carrehey
Robert del Bothe
Thomas Emottez, junior
William, son of Thos. Emottez
John Hertley
Henry Hertley
John, son of Robert Hertley
Geoffrey Hertley
Robert Hertley
John Hertely

We have looked at Wycoller as it existed in the middle ages—its place within a royal forest, its cattle-rearing and its sufferings from national problems. We have, in conclusion, discovered the names of the early inhabitants. The predominance of the Hartley family had already made itself very evident, and we shall see that this trend continued in Tudor Times.

Origin of the name

The earliest spellings of Wycoller were Wycolure in 1324, Wyculure in 1325, Over-wycolur and Nether Wycolur in 1423 and Over wicoller and Netherwicoller in 1464. In Tudor times the name was spelt in a variety of ways depending on the interpretation of the clerk or cleric who wrote it down. As the spelling has altered so much it is unlikely to be a reliable guide to the meaning of the name. The phonetic pronunciation on the other hand is far more likely to give a clue.

In *The Place Names of Lancashire* Dr. E. Eckwall says that the name Wycoller seems to be a compound of the Old English "wic" and "alr" (alder), the former in this case very likely referring to a dairy farm. "Wic" can be a dwelling, a building or collection of buildings, a farm or a dairy farm. But as Wycoller is a small place and was even smaller when it gained its name, "wic" very probably referred simply to a farm or dairy farm. E. W. Folley gives a further explanation in *Romantic Wycoller*.

> *Its name would appear to spring from "Wic" meaning a community, "col" narrow, and "dwr" water, combining to make a "Colder" or "Calder", the whole forming "the community on the narrow water", . . . There is another possible derivation. The Anglo Saxon word "Cwic" means living or evergreen, "Alr" for "alder" is another Saxon word, and "Cwicalr" may refer to the ready springing of alders which abound in all the length of the Dene.*

The original meaning may still have alluded us, but the theory that the name is derived from a dairy farm among the alders is the one most widely accepted today.

Tudor Times

In August 1485 Henry Tudor won the day and the throne of England at Bosworth Field. Richard III who had murdered his way to the throne was killed and carried from the field naked and dead across the back of a horse. The House of Tudor was established.

The immediate effect on the inhabitants of Wycoller was slight, but it was the new king Henry VII who was to be the instigator of great changes in the Forest of Trawden. During the fifteenth century there had been slight but progressive improvement in Wycoller, the two vaccaries had been let on lease, and the tenants and their families were developing their farmsteads. The improvement of the old vaccary land is probably reflected in the increased rent charges. The Trawden Forest vaccaries worth £2. 8s. 0d. in 1323 had increased to £21. 13s. 4d. by 1423 and further increases came later in the century.

It is said that Henry VII was the best business man to sit on the English throne; having no wish to be a victim of royal poverty he was determined to make a financial success of things, and his economic policies made themsleves felt in the tiny hamlet of Wycoller. From initial debt he built up royal wealth that exceeded all previous reigns. Henry commanded a survey of all his lands in Blackburnshire, and following the survey a decree was issued dated 12 March 1507. This decree was entered in the court rolls for the Halmot held at Colne on Friday 28 May 1507.

A Decree of our Lord the King, under the Seal of his Duchy of Lancaster, to his Steward of Blackburnshir, in the said county, directed in these words:-
HENRY, *by the grace of God, King of England and of ffraunce, and Lord of Ireland, To our trusty and wellbeloved the Stuards that now is and that hereafter schalbe of our posessions of Blackburne, within our countie palatyne of Lancastre, greting. Forsomuch as heretofore we, by our letters of commission, under our seale of our Duchie of Lancastre, late deputied and apoynted Sir John Bothe and other to vieu and survey all our honours, castelles and lordsippes within our said counte palatyne, and thereupon to do emprowe the same, and every parcell of them for our most singler profite & advantage, whereupon we understand that our said Commissioners have*

endevorid themself surveing and approving the same according to our said commission & pleasure, and have made grauntes and promises of leases of certeyn of our landes and tenements within our said countie, according to the tenure and effecte of a cedule to theis our letter annexed, to certyne persones, to have and holde to theym and to their heires for time of lyve or lyves, or for terme of yeres, after the custom of the Manor, by cope of Court Rolle, for execucion and accomplysshment whereof we have autorised, and by their presentes auctorise and gif unto you full auctorite and power by theis our letters calling unto you the said Sir John Bothe, and by his advice to set and let all such of our landes and tenementes as be or ley within your said office to the said persones, for suche rentes yerly as be conteyned in the said cedule; To have and holde to them and to their heires or otherwise, for terme of lyve or yeres, at the libertie and choyse of our said tennantes, infor the full accomplisshment of the said promisses and grauntes taking sufficient surtie of the said personnes for the sure payment of the same rent as ye shall seme best and most convenient; And also that upon the deth or chaunge of every tennant that ye shall make newe lease or leases to such persone or persones as afor the deth or chaunge of eny suche tennant or tennantes as the same landes shall happen to be graunted to by you, Takyng of every suche tennant as schall happen to chaunge or decease oon hole yeres Rent of the same tennantre that ye shall nowe take for a fyne, according as other our tennants there, being copyholders tyme out of mynde, have usyyd to pay in such cases over and above their auncyene and olde yerely Rent of the same: Providing and allway forseen that ye, by color of your said leases do not diminysshe our said Rentes, fynes and gressoms, ne our other duties due and demandable for us in that partie, and thies our letters schalbe unto you at all tymes sufficient warrant and discharge in this behalfe; which our letters we woll that ye do entre into our Court Rolles, ther to remayn of record for the more sueritie of every of our said tennant for their said leases to be had and made accordinglie.

Geven at our Citie of London, under the Seale of our said Duchie, the xij. day of Marche, the xxij. yere of our reigne. By the Council of the said Duchy.

This royal decree, coming between the surrender of land and complaints of trespass was a landmark in the development of Trawden Forest and the other forests of Blackburnshire. This was the

'Grauntinge of the Forrests'

'Grauntinge of the Forrests' now commonly referred to as the disafforestation. The term disafforestation suggests that there was immediate and energetic activity in chopping down the forest trees. In fact the change was in the spirit rather than immediate action. At last the inhabitants of the forest were to be considered above the deer. They had previously been afraid to deal effectively with deer that trespassed and damaged their crops. Now slowly and surely land was better fenced, more waste land was cleared, and the forest and its animals were on the retreat.

Before the disafforestation of Trawden Forest Woodmotes were held twice a year at Colne. These courts dealt with all matters concerning the forest and its inhabitants. After the disafforestation a jury of twelve inhabitants of the forest, comprised of men from Trawden, Winewall and Wycoller went to Colne where an Inquisition was held. The first Inquisition were held along with the Halmot of Colne and often the business of these two courts was intermixed. The meetings were held twice yearly on Tuesday a month after Easter and Michaelmas. All males from their teens to the age of sixty years were obliged to attend court and on first joining the court they took a rhymed oath as a pledge of loyalty.

At the court complaints were heard, land was transferred and fines were enforced for a variety of misdemeanours, such as brewing without licence, playing unlawful games, allowing cattle to stray and generally interfering with neighbours' land and fences. The records of these courts were preserved at Clitheroe Castle and many of them were transcribed from the original Latin by William Farrer in the eighteen nineties. A study of these records gives an interesting picture of Wycoller folk at the time. When the first Inquisition of the Forest of Trawden was held on 28 May 1510, the jury presented Thomas Emmott for trespassing with his cattle in Wycoller and he was fined 4d. The following year on 22 March 1511, James Foulds was fined for letting his horse trespass in Wycoller and John Helynthrop for trespassing there in both summer and winter with three horses and other animals. Trespassing, that is allowing animals to graze on private or common land to which they had no claim, was a fineable offence. Allowing a beast to wander loose was also a trespass, the beast was placed in the pinfold, usually simply referred to as the fold in Trawden Forest, and the owner had to pay a fine for its release. Occasionally the owner would free his own animals from the fold but for this he usually suffered a heavier fine. In 1546 the court rolls record that "Nicolas Herteley, Roger son of Richard Herteley, and Roger Hertely, alias Lityll Hoge, trespass within Beardsheybothe with their animals; and that Roger, son of the said Richard Herteley of Trawden, John and Gilbert Hertely broke the King's Fold in Trawden, and removed thence their animals without license". All those concerned were fined but the guilty ones who broke the fold were fined double.

The transfer of land was probably the most important item dealt with in the court. The people held their land as copyholders and on the death of a copyholder the land reverted to the Lord of the Manor. However, the eldest son or widow was allowed to continue occupation on the immediate transfer payment of one years' rent. One of the first transfers of Wycoller land was recorded on 30 April 1521 "j. messuage, with the appurtenances, lying in Wycolers, yearly rent xxjs, has reverted to the King, by the death of Peter Hertley, senior, and that John Hertley is his son and next heir. Cecily, widow of the said Peter, forbad fine for her dower right. The said John then found John Shackilton and John Hanson as sureties to reply. Admittance granted: fine, xxjs". Peter Hartley had died and here we see that his son John took over the 'messuage' which was a farm with outbuildings. Cecily, the widow, "forbad a fine for her dower right", which means that she claimed her widow's portion of one quarter of the farm's income during her lifetime. This matter having been settled the son was then officially granted the land on payment of 21s.

In 1525 the court rolls record: "It is presented by the inquisition taken from the Forest of Trawden, that j. messuage and the appurtenances, in Wicoler, ixs annual rent, have reverted to the King, by the death of James Folds, and that John ffolds is his son and next heir. Caterine, widow of the said James Folds forbids fine for her dower. The said John finds surety Geoffrey Folds and Christopher Hertley, and is admitted, fine ixs".

In 1537 a squabble over inheritance led to those concerned being called to Bolling Hall, near Bradford by Sir Richard Tempest

> *That Where as contravers, stryvez and debaitts is had and moved betwix John Herteley, thelder son of Peter Herteley of Wycoler apon the one partye, and Geofferey Herteley, younger son of the said Peter, apon the other partyre, of, for and cons'nyng on surrender to be mayd by the seyd Peter Hertely, their Father, in, of and apon his hole messuages and Buyldyngs, lands and medows, mores and pasturs, set, lyyng and Beyng in Wycoller, Within the fforest and*

33

> *Chase of Trawden, of the yerely Kyngs rent of xxxs, the wiche the seyd Peter now standyth sole Fyned and seased of by copye of Cowrte Rolle to hym and to his heires accordyng to the custome and manor of Colne, and now clamed by bothe the seids John Hertely and Geofferey Hertely, sonnes of the seyd Peter Hertely . . . Sir Richard Tempest, Knyght, beyng heid stuard of Blackburnshir under the Kyngs maiestye . . . callyng the seyd John Hertely and Geofferey Hertely . . . afore hym at Bollyng Hall . . . after delyberat hearyng . . . ordered and determyned that the seyd Peter Herteley, the Father, Imedyatly, ffurthwith, within a convenyent tyme . . . shuld surrender and gyff upp all his seyd meses . . . into the Grave of Trawden his hands, to the use and behove of Roger Herteley, called Lyttil Hoge, Bernard Hertely, son of Xpofer Hertely, Geffery ffolds, and James Hertely, and their heires, as Feoffes in trust, And they to make their Fyne at the hands of the Stuard . . . and so shall stond Fyned and seased in, of, and apon the seyds meses . . . to the use of the seid Peter for terme of his lyff, and after his decease of the moyte of the seids mesez and buyldyngs, with halff of all the seyds lands, medows, mores, commons, and pasturs, of the yerely rent of xvs, to the use & behove of John Hertely thelder, sonne of the seid Peter Herteley, And to the heires of the bodye of the seid John lawfully begotten, and lykewise the seid Roger and his cofeoffes and their heires to stond fyned and seased apon the other moyte . . . to the use of Gefferey Hertely, yonger son of the seid Peter, and to the heires of his bodye lawfully begotten . . . and for defalfth of such Isshews of the bodyes bothe of the seid John and Gefferey Heteley . . . to the use and behove of the next heires of the seid Peter Herteley for ever . . . . Yeven at Bowlyng afforeseid, by the seyd Sir Richard Tempest Knyght, the Eight day of May, in the xviij yere of the reigne of our Soverand lord Kyng Henry the Eight.*

With considerable frequency the inhabitants of Wycoller complained against the inhabitants of Winewall for encroaching onto their lands or for some similar alleged offence. In 1516 there were claims and counter claims from both townships.

> *Roger Hertlay of Wynewall, Geoffrey Dryver, and other tenants in Wynewall, complain against Peter Hertlay senior, Peter Hertlay, junior, Peter Folds, Christopher Hertlay, junior, Richard Emmott, and Christopher Hertlay, senior, in a plea of trespass, in treading down and wasting their meadow and pasture grass with their beasts to their injury in the sum of xls.*

Knowing that the complaint was coming, the Wycoller tenants were ready with their own charges and as the inhabitants of Winewall were claiming 11s. damages they claimed £11.

> *Peter Hertlay and other tenants of Wycoler complain against the said Roger Hertlay and other tenants of Wynewall aforesaid, in a plea of detenue of the yearly agistment in Over-Wycoler and Nether-Wycoler for ten years past—to wit, for each year one mark—to their injury in the sum of xl li; and for detenue of a yearly rent of xxvjs—viijd from Over-Wycoler and Nether-Wycoler, whereby the said plaintiffs have suffered loss.*

In the first case the hearing was postponed and in the second case no verdict was recorded. At times a special jury of twenty-four jurors from Trawden, Pendle and Rossendale was called to settle troublesome land disputes. Such a case occurred in 1527.

> *Roger Hertley, senior, Roger Herteley, junior, and other tenants of our lord the King in Trawden, complain against Christopher Hertley, senior of Wicoler, and other tenants there, and John Hartley of Wynewall and other tenants there, in a plea of detenue and occupation of certain lands lying in Trawden, called Deipeclogh, Greithill, and Ollerbarrow, to the injury of the said plaintiffs in the sum of x li. A jury of xxiiij customers of the Forests of Trawden Pendil and Rossendale, declare that the defendants are not guilty of the charge, and that the premises in no way belong to the said plaintiffs.*

The last case we look at came from the same court held at Colne on 1 October 1572.

> *Christopher Herteley and John Herteley of Wicoler, and other tenants, being their neighbours, complain against Roger Hertley and Roger Hertley [sic], and others their neighbours, in a plea of trespass and damages from bad fences, to their injury in the sum of xx li.*

In this case no verdict was given as, according to the rolls, "neither party produced any evidence, either by word or writ".

In 1507 Roger Hartley and others were fined for selling beer

35

Over the centuries stone was the basic material in which Wycoller expressed itself. A heavy stone lintel from Wycoller Hall

"Take wete and pyke hit fayre and clene, and do it in a mortar shene". This is the first part of a centuries old recipe for the making of a once-popular dish frumenty or furmety made with wheat and milk

Inscribed potion of a mortar from Wycoller Beck

Stone cross from the foundations of Wycoller Cottage

without a stamped measure; the sale of food and drink was, clearly, kept under strict control. The court had a duty to "enquire of Brewers and Typlers whether they made good and wholesome ale and beere for man's body, or not, and sell and utter the same according to the lawes and statutes of this Realme. And also they ought not to put out their signe or ale-stake until their ale be asseyed by the ale-taster, and then sell, and not before".

Rogues and vagabonds

The courts were also charged to look out for rogues, and those likely to be rogues were said to be, "Procters of Spittlehouses, Patent—gatherers, or Collectors for Gaoles, prisons, or Hospitals, Fencers, Bearwards, common Plaiers of enterludes, Minstrils wandring abroad. Glassemen, Saylers, Souldiers, Schollers, and all other idle persons which goe about begging". Wycoller seems to have had little trouble with rogues as most of them appear to have lived in Colne.

Unlawful games

People were not allowed to play unlawful games and the jury were charged to "inquire if any Alehousekeeper or other person do keepe any unlawfull games in his or their house or houses, or elsewhere, as cards, dice, tables, loggets, quoits, bowles, or such like". This list seems fairly comprehensive and allows little scope for playing any games at all. The exception was, "in the Christmas time; for then all men may play". Unfortunately the locals could rarely wait for Christmas and were frequently fined as in June 1557 when a larger number of people including John Hartley and Peter Hartley of Wycoller were fined for having "played at a certain unlawful and prohibited game called the scoles". It would be interesting to know exactly what this game was.

On a few occasions there was nothing for the jurors to do as in April 1523 when they were able to declare, "that in Trawden Forest all is well". In May 1544 the Jury at the Inquisition taken from the Forest of Trawden had nothing to present, and on a third occasion in 1555 the rolls record, "Inquisition taken from the Forest of Trawden by the oath of the jury, who say that within the said Forest all things are well".

Unfortunately the court rolls rarely give sufficient information for full family trees to be drawn up as they were not made or preserved for future genealogists and historians but for settlement of land disputes. That this was necessary is shown in 1549 when John Hartley of Wycoller complained that he had been cheated out of part of the Wycoller vaccary land left to him by his father. The defendants denied the charge of fraudulence and asked "for production of the

Roll in support of their defence". The evidence of the court rolls was considered by the jury and John lost his case. Occasionally some field names and other land descriptions are given, but buildings in Wycoller are never named in the Tudor court rolls. In 1548 "John ffoldes of Wycoller complains against John Hertely of Wycoller, and James son of Roger Herteley, in a plea of trespass, viz., of obstructing a way commencing at a gap called the Flodyait, descending the Hempelandes, and from thence to a parcel of land called 'le Swynecroft', and across the Synecroft Forthe, as far as a close called 'le Westsyde de le Hey".

Probate records   From Tudor times only a few wills of Wycoller folk survive, yet, with careful transcription and a little study, it is surprising what these probate documents can tell us of the day-to-day lives of the people who made them all those centuries ago. They will often provide a list of the testator's family and relations which allows us to make at least a brief family tree. Elizabeth Emmott's will of 1597 tells us that she was a widow and that her eldest son Robert was also dead. We learn that her son Robert had two daughters, Elizabeth and Ellen, to whom she left the majority of her possessions. However, by far the most interesting information comes from the rather dry looking inventory which was appended to the will before it was finally proved. This list of possessions was drawn up after death by reliable local people and included all the deceased's goods and chattels excluding real estate.

Elizabeth Emmott's inventory tells us a great deal about her style of life. She was principally a yeoman farmer's widow who had carried on the farm after her husband's death. Women certainly had an inferior status in Tudor days and their freedom was very much restricted. It was only as a widow that Elizabeth could enjoy relative equality with men. She had twenty-eight cattle, including four oxen used for ploughing and pulling the farm carts. The list shows only one pig, and from other Trawden Forest inventories it appears that pigs were usually kept in small numbers. Elizabeth had no horses, which is surprising, but there is no reason why she should not have hired a horse for any necessary journey. Her neighbour, Roger Hartley of Wycoller, who died in 1589, had several horses as well as eight or ten oxen.

Both Elizabeth Emmott and Roger Hartley, whose will was proved in 1589, had both ploughs, plough irons and plenty of other "husbandrie geare". The village had to be self-sufficient and a variety of crops had to be grown, although the main crops were oats and barley. Elizabeth had "Meale, malte, groates and duste", worth £3 and Roger Hartley had "ote meale and malte", worth £2. Oats was the main crop in the North of England followed by barley, much of the latter being used for brewing the staple drink of the time.

Apart from supplying their own needs a village often produced a surplus of some crop or produce which could be sold to the outside world and bring in extra money to raise the standard of living. Wycoller's extra produce was cloth. Probably since Norman times sheep had been kept in the valley, and certainly from the thirteenth century there were local fulling stocks to treat the cloth which was produced in the cottage and farm. The sheep that supplied the wool fed on the upland pastures of Trawden Forest; lean sheep feeding on lean pasture but the wool was good for weaving.

Elizabeth Emmott had one hundred and twenty sheep and Roger Hartley had well over two hundred. Elizabeth had no looms in the house but she had "fleeces and broken wole"; Roger had "two peyre of lomes", that is two looms, and "cardes, wheles and comes" for preparing the raw wool, he had also both wool and linen cloth. At this time weaving went along with farming as a supporting occupation. The fleeces were spread on the floor, and the women and children would pick out the sticks and dirt. The wool was sprinkled with oil and then carded, that is teased into a light floss by hand cards. After carding the wool was ready for spinning. By this time the distaff was out but most families had at least one spinning wheel. Spinning was done by all the women of the family from aunts to grown up daughters. It was a slow job and those who specialised in cloth making rather than farming would get their spinning done by poorer neighbours.

Tudor weaving

After spinning, the yarn was processed to make it easier to handle. First it was dipped in a stream to wash it and then it was "wuzzed" to get rid of the water. The wet yarn was placed in a basket at the end of a stick, the stick being supported in a "wuzzin hole" while the basket was flung round and round and the water extracted. Once dry the yarn was ready for weaving which was work for the older boys and men of the family. The Tudor handloom had no flying shuttle and weaving was a slow process.

The woven cloth still had many processes to go through although it was often sold in the unfinished state. The first process often

A true Inventorie of all and singular the goods cattells debts substance and somes of money movable and immovable of Elizabeth Emott late of Wicoler in the countie of Lancaster widowe deceased Seene and prysed by John Emott of Emott James Hertley of Wicoler James Emott of the same and Lawrence Emott of Barnesett the xxv th day of Auguste Anno regni dne Elizabeth dei gra Anglia ffrance et hiberne fides defensor tricecessimo nono Anno dni 1597 as followethe

Imprimis fower oxen three steeres and fower twinters	£32.	0s.	0d.
Item sixe kyne and two whyes	£17.	0s.	0d.
Item fower stirkes and three calves	£5.	0s.	0d.
Item fyve score and one old sheepes and xx lambes	£18	0s.	0d.
Item one fatt Cowe and one swyne	£3.	6s.	8d.
Item in waynes wheles yockes teames and other things bilonginge to husbandrie	£2.	0s.	0d.
Item in plowes plowe irons pickes mells wedges gavelockes harrowes huckes shelves spades one wimble and other implements	£1.	10s.	0d.
Item in Arkes chistes and one table	£7.	0s.	0d.
Item in Bedstockes	£1.	13s.	4d.
Item in Coverlettes blankettes sheets & beddinge	£9.	0s.	0d.
Item in sackes and window clothes	£1.	0s.	0d.
Item in pannes pottes pewther & brasen vessells	£3.	15s.	0d.
Item in wodd vessells fleeces & broken wole	£4.	4s.	0d.
Item in meale malte groates and duste	£3.	0s.	0d.
Item in fleshe butter and cheese	£1.	18s.	0d.
Item in cheares stoles & cuschions	£0.	16s.	0d.
Item two counters with other bordes & formes	£0.	10s.	0d.
Item one chymney recontrie and tonges	£0.	10s.	0d.
Item her apparell with other raymentes of clothes	£2.	0s.	0d.

Item turves and other hustlementes and

40

A true Inventorie Indented of all and singuler the goods Cattells debts substance and somes of money moveable and Immoveable of Elizabeth Emott late of Wroley in the countie of Lancaster widowe deceassed seene and vysed by John Emott of Emott sand of Chadley of Wroley James Emott of her same and Lawrence Emott of Burnsall the __ day of August Anno regni dne Elizabethe dei gra Anglie Francie et hibine fidei defensor &c tricessimo nono Anno dni 1597 as followeth

In primis fower oxen three steeres and fower twinters — xxiijli
Item sex kyne and two whyes — xvijli
Item sex keyne and two calves — vli
Item fower stirks and three calves — viijli
Item hye stote and one olde sheepe and xx lambes — iijli vjs viijd
Item one fatt cowe and one Rynte —
Item in wagnes woles yorke teames and other thinge belonginge to husbandrie — xls
Item in plowes plowe frene yirke mettle wedge gavelocke harrowes barke sholes — vijs
spades one rimble and other implementes
Item in duke chiste and one table — vijli
Item in bedsteke — xxviij iiij
Item coverlette blankette sheetes & beddinge — xli
Item in barke and window clothes — xxli
Item in panned pottes pewder & brason vessell — iijli xs
Item woodvessell flaures & broken wold — iijli iiijs
Item in meale malte grotes and duste — iijli
Item in flesse butter and chese — xxxiiijs
Item in chares stoles & cusshions — vijs
Item two roundles wolser bordes & soundes — xs
Item one chimney yrondire and tonge — xs
Item her appell wolser ragment of clothes — xls
Item cubbes and other husleme and ont shep — iijli iiijs
and her somme ette of one Rybe — iijli xs iiijs
Item in gonts tem mondy — iiijs xijs iiijs
Item corne and hay — vli

Debts owinge unto they said deceased
Imprimis by Roger Chadley of Poynewald — xviijs vj iiijs
Item by Nicholas Withers and Margrett his wyffe — viijs
Item by willm Emott — vijs ijs
Item by Willm Clawretter — vijs
Item by John Chadley — ijs upon accompts to lys

one hyde and the fourte parte of one
hyve   £0. 13s. 4d.
Item in goulde and money   £53. 16s. 4d.
Item corne and hay   £15.   0s. 0d.

    Debte owinge unto the saied deceased
Imprimis by Roger Hartley of Wynewale   £17. 6s. 8d.
Item by Nicholas Mitchell and Margrett
his wife   £12. 0s. 0d.

Wuzzin yarn at Pearson's Farm

Wuzzin holes in the wall of Pearson's Farm

Item by William Emott	£7. 10s. 0d.
Item by William Hargreves	£8. 0s. 0d.
Item by John Hartley	£9. 0s. 0d.

---

involved treating it with the urine of animals and humans, the latter being collected from lant troughs in various parts of the village. Another of the processes took place at the fulling mill. The earliest method of fulling cloth was by trampling the cloth underfoot, but from the thirteenth century fulling stocks were used. These stocks were two heavy wooden hammers, which were lifted by tappets on the axle of a water wheel and allowed to fall onto the wet soapy cloth in the trough below. At each fall of the hammers the cloth rotated in the trough causing it to thicken and the warp and weft to become well meshed together. Finally the cloth was put on tenting frames to stretch and dry and Wycoller still has its "Tenter Field", the long narrow field that stretches from the top of the bank above the packhorse bridge, on the Hall side, to Height Laithe on the Haworth road.

The slow process of a hand shuttle before the advent of Kay's Flying Shuttle

Lant trough at Wycoller Cottage

The cloth was often sold direct from the loom and the final process was completed by the buyer. Some cloth was finished by having its hairs or "nap" raised by teasels and then cut evenly by the great shears of the cloth finisher. It must be remembered that the processes in cloth making varied from time to time, from cloth to cloth, from village to village, and even from family to family, so that any short account must unfortunately give a very limited picture.

In 1598 when William Hargreaves of Wycoller died he was styled a clothier, showing that in Tudor Wycoller there were those who specialised in cloth production. Regretfully his will has no inventory attached to it and so are we unable to fully estimate the extent of his involvement in the cloth trade. It is interesting to note that the will of Elizabeth Emmott of 1597 names him as one of the guardians of her grand daughters, Elizabeth and Ellen Emmott. Unfortunately William's guardianship was cut short as he died the year following.

Food   The probate inventories give us a good idea what the people of Wycoller ate in Tudor times. They had, "flesche, butter and cheese", "byff and bacon" and plenty of oats, groats, corn and malt. As most inventories contain a backstone it can be assumed that oatcake was part of the staple diet. Roger Hartley kept hens and so both eggs and poultry were likely to be included in his diet. The sides of bacon would hang in the larder, suspended from the iron hooks still to be found in many country farmhouses, and the beef was likely to have been salted in the tub. However, both winter and summer inventories show that the people had roughly the same amount of meat in stock at all times of the year. This supports the early evidence of the vaccaries that cattle were only slaughtered as meat was needed and that wholesale slaughter for the winter is to a great extent a long-sustained myth. Wycoller folk had their barns well-stocked with hay and corn, and although their cattle would be far leaner than their descendants today they were provided for throughout the winter.

It has often been said that life for farm and cottage folk in Tudor times was rough, dirty and uncomfortable. The daily routine was hard by our standards but to those living at the time things were better than they had ever been, and for the yeoman farmers of Wycoller the standard of living was slowly rising. Most farms like Elizabeth Emmott's had "cheares, stoles and cuschions" and we should not imagine Tudor folk sitting on the bare boards of furniture such as we see in museums like Towneley Hall, in their day they would have been well-cushioned.

Home comforts

The Tudor folk also took care of their night-time comfort. By the latter part of Elizabeth's reign the days of straw beds were going and people had considerable value in their beds and bedding. Elizabeth Emmott had "coverlettes, blankettes, sheetes and beddinge" worth £9 apart from the beds themselves. William Harrison an Elizabethan parson, recorded the improvement in household conditions in Tudor times stressing that it affected all levels of society.

> *Our fathers yea we ourselves have lien full oft upon straw pallets, covered only with a sheet, under coverlets of dagswain or hop harlots and a good round log under their heads instead of a bolster. If it were so that our fathers or the good man of the house has a matress or flockbed and thereto a sack of chaff to rest his head upon, he thought himself to be as well lodged as the lord of the town, that peradventure lay seldom in a bed of down or whole feathers. Pillows were thought meet only for women in childbirth. As for servants, if they had any sheet above them, it was well, for seldom had they any under their bodies, to keep them from the pricking straws that ran oft through the canvas of the pallet and razed their hardened hides.*

Harrison also noted that with the greater use of coal, chimneys had become common during the Elizabethan period, as coal smoke was far more disagreeable than that of wood. This suggests that a great many sixteenth century houses had no chimney as we know it. The Wycoller inventories show the possession of fire-irons and the use of both peat and coal as fuel.

The earliest named inhabitants of Wycoller were Hartleys. In 1416 the tenants of the two vaccaries were Geoffrey Hartley and Robert Hartley and they were still the tenants in 1432. In 1443 the tenants of Winewall and Wycoller vaccaries were Robert de Bothe, John Hartley, Geoffrey Hartley, Thomas Emmott, Henry Hartley, Robert Hartley, William son of Thomas Emmott, John Hartley and John son of Robert Hartley.

Hartley, Hartley everywhere!

The Hartley family in Trawden Forest are a genealogist's nightmare. Prolific in the extreme they spread throughout the Forest and into surrounding areas. As conservative as they were prolific they tended to keep to the same few Christian names such as James, Peter, John, Roger and Christopher. When the jurors sat at the Inquisition for the Forest of Trawden it must have been almost a family affair. In October 1510 the jury were, "Lawrence Robert, Roger Hertley, sen., Geoffrey Dryver, James Hertley, Roger Hertley jun., Hugh Hertley, Geoffrey Hertley, William Hertley, Christopher Hertley, Richard Shackylden, Roger Hertley and John Hertley of Trawden". Nine of the twelve jury-men were Hartleys. Not only were they the main body of the jury but Hartley business, Hartley misdemeanours and Hartley land squabbles took up the main part of the court's time.

The Hartleys being so numerous and their Christian names so limited it often gave rise to confusion. Fathers' names had to be given to help with identification especially when business was committed to paper. In 1608, when the tenants of the newhold were listed 60% of Wycoller tenants, 50% of Winewall tenants, and 70% of those in Trawden were Hartleys. The locals solved the problem with nicknames and these nicknames are frequently recorded in the court transactions.

There was John Hartley known as Byrdye, and Roger Hartley known as Little Hog, Roger Hartley alias Pynnes or Pynne, John Hartley called Pyenose and John Hartley called Hoydye. As ever some of the nicknames were far from complimentary but they were not only used in conversation but also in official documents. A little imagination will suggest characters that led to such nicknames as Little Hog, Byrdye, Pyenose and Pynnes. Hoydye does not seem so obvious but the fact that hoy is a cattle call may be a sign of its origin or it could well be a corruption of Odd Eye as many of the nicknames refer to unusual physical features.

The Hartleys are part of the historical skeleton of Trawden Forest, occurring from time to time but with monotonous regularity. They must have been a fertile clan especially in producing sons to continue the family, although occasionally they did lose land when a landowning Hartley had only daughters—indeed it was marriage to a Hartley heiress that gave the Cunliffes their foothold in Wycoller.

Stuart Period

Early in the reign of the first Stuart sovereign, James I, the inhabitants of Wycoller and all other people living in the Forests of Blackburnshire received a severe blow. The opening of the Tudor period, over a century earlier, had brought the Commission for Granting of the Forests: uncultivated land had been granted to various tenants and they had become copyholders, holding their lands on the titles founded on the commission. That the titles were genuine and uncontrovertable was never doubted. Houses and farmsteads had been erected, land had been cleared and tilled, some land had been sold, and the majority of holdings had been passed from father to son several times. In 1607, however, the Crown lawyers discovered what they declared to be a defective title on the part of the copyholders. This discovery was set out in a letter dated 5 April 1607 and was addressed to Mr. Auditor Fanshaw, and Ralph Asheton of Lever, Esq., deputy steward.

> *There are within his Majesty's honor of Clitheroe, divers lands which have been only granted by the steward, and by warrant to the steward made, which parcels have been improved out of his majesty's forests and chases, there commonley called lands of the new-hold, which are only, however, of the nature of essart land, and cannot be claimed by custom or prescription to be copyholds.*

This came as a thunderstroke and affected the title to twenty-five thousand acres of land in Lancashire. It destroyed the hopes and stability of many families who had no other means of support than the land they held. There was lengthy litigation but the outcome was a demand from the Crown for further payments to be made by copyholders to ensure the perfecting of their title to their lands. It is difficult to imagine a more bare-faced attempt to extort money under false pretences.

In spite of the injustice of the claim many local landowners were still keen to ingratiate themselves with James and his ministers because they were afraid of losing their lands. Although they themselves were willing to pay they found it impossible to persuade the smaller yeoman farmers to join them. A letter from Richard Towneley, Edward Rausthorn, and others, makes the case clear.

Through the fantastical persuasion of the vulgar sorte, that handes set to an instrument will bind them to they know not what inconveniences, they are enforced to rest only on promises: now in respect the vulgar sorte is known to be variable, and may alter from this second resolution; least the peevishness of some few should disadvantage or discredit our undertaking; we are of opinion that this, by Mr. Auditor's and your good meanes made known to the privy council, will worke such effect, yet according to ye proverbe, 'The fryers shall not be beaten for the nunnes fault'.

Here in this letter the local gentry attempted to get out of the difficulty by currying favour and blaming the obstinacy and stupidity of 'the vulgar sorte'. However, it was 'the vulgar sorte' who made their objections and stood firm, showing the true spirit of English yeomen guarding their traditional rights. The matter was eventually settled and the tenants were given a number of years in which to pay the money demanded. The copyholders of Wycoller in 1608 were John Hartley, Roger Hartley, James Hartley, Peter Hartley, Robert Emmott and Elizabeth his wife, John Foulds, and John Emmott.

Portion of the map of Lancashire prepared by John Speed in 1610

The Cunliffe family

In August 1611 Nicholas Cunliffe and Elizabeth Hartley were married at the parish church in Colne. Nicholas was a member of the Cunliffe family of Hollins near Accrington and Elizabeth was one of the Wycoller Hartleys. After the marriage the couple settled at Wycoller and their children are entered in the baptismal registers at Colne.

Nicholas Cunliffe m. 19 Aug. 1611
Elizabeth Hartley

bap.	bap.	bap.	bap.	bap.
14 Sept.	11 Oct.	30 Sept.	18 July	4 Feb.
1612	1618	1621	1623	1627
John	Nicholas	Ellis	Robert	Elizabeth

With this marriage of Nicholas and Elizabeth Hartley the Cunliffe family first enter our story. From this time until the death of Henry Owen Cunliffe in 1818 the Cunliffes played an important part in the story of the village of Wycoller, and even now, a century after their family seat became a ruin, members of various branches of this family scattered throughout England and the New World still retain a nostalgic connection with the moorland village of their ancestors.

More nonsense has been written about this family than most in Lancashire and its printed pedigrees are as unreliable as any. The pedigrees in Gregson's *Portfolio of Fragments*, Whitaker's *History of Whalley* and others are riddled with errors and omissions. Research, considerable time and patience, some travel and a family interest should make it possible to produce a reliable Cunliffe pedigree from the sixteenth century, but we must leave that to the Cunliffes, as here we are concerned only with the Cunliffe family as they influenced Wycoller.

Nicholas Cunliffe's eldest son John is said to have married Grace Hartley on 8 December 1628. A daughter Elizabeth was baptised on 15 November 1635 at Colne parish church, but she survived only until September the following year. The mother Grace had died even earlier in March 1636, both mother and daughter were buried at Colne. John Cunliffe is said to have married again in April 1638, and his second wife was Mary Chetham daughter of

Ralph Chetham of Manchester. This marriage was blessed with eleven children of which only Nicholas, baptised at Colne in 1640, the eldest son, was born at Wycoller. John Cunliffe is said to have moved to Hollins at this period.

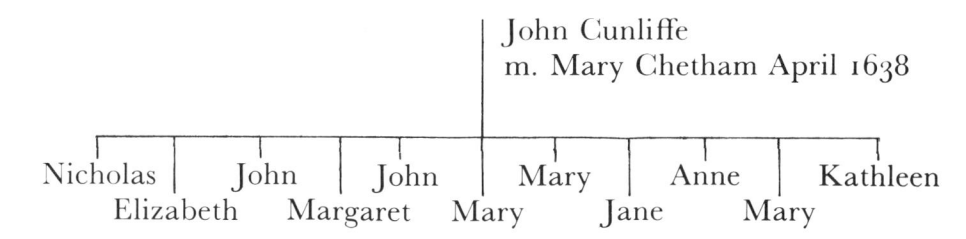

```
                        John Cunliffe
                        m. Mary Chetham April 1638
   ┌────────┬──────────┬────────┬────────┬────────┬──────────┐
 Nicholas   John       John     Mary     Anne     Kathleen
 Elizabeth  Margaret   Mary     Jane     Mary
```

Nicholas Cunliffe was present at the Preston Guild of 1622 and again in 1642 at which time he entered himself, his four sons and his grandson upon the Guild Roll. They were, John, Nicholas, Ellis, Robert and grandson Nicholas the son of John. That same year of 1642 England was thrown into turmoil by Civil War.

The rift between Charles I and Parliament had widened and conflict had become inevitable. In Lancashire the gentry and officers of the trained bands met together at Preston in June 1642 to decide whether they should fight for King or Parliament. It was impossible for common agreement to be reached and the meeting broke up in some disorder. The Hundred of Blackburn, which included Marsden, Colne and Trawden supported Parliament, but a large part of Lancashire including the important towns of Preston and Lancaster supported the King's cause. The Parliamentarian forces in Lancashire were put under the control of Richard Shuttleworth of Gawthorpe Hall who together with his son Richard was a Lancashire member of Parliament. The Royalist forces were commanded by Lord Derby.

Civil War

Fighting began when the Royalists unsuccessfully attacked Manchester in the summer, but it was not until October 1642 that Richard Shuttleworth called a meeting to organise the local militia in Blackburnshire and to appoint local officers. Nicholas Cunliffe of Wycoller attended this meeting and was appointed one of the four captains of the Colne troops; the others being John Bannister, Daniel Bernard and John Hammond. The initial attack came from Sir Gilbert Hoghton who captured Blackburn with his Royalist forces. On 20 October Richard Shuttleworth defeated the Royalists at Clayton-le-Moors following which he re-captured Blackburn. A report of the engagement says, "Now the men of Blackburn, Padiham, Burnley, Clitheroe and Colne with those sturdy churls in the two forests of Pendle and Rossendale have roused their spirits and have resolved to fight it out rather than their beef and bacon be taken from them". This report fails to mention Trawden Forest but there would surely have been some 'sturdy churls' from Trawden, Winewall and Wycoller, along with Captain Nicholas Cunliffe.

The year 1643 was a year of great activity. In February Richard Shuttleworth received reinforcements from Manchester and soon Lancaster and Preston fell into their hands. However, they did not hold these towns for very long as in March they were re-captured by Lord Derby. In April Lord Derby moved on to Blackburn and Ribchester and camped at Whalley on 19 April. It appears that most of the Parliamentary forces had returned to their farms and had speedily to be recalled.

On the evening of 19 April a hurried meeting was called at Gawthorpe to decide what action should be taken. The Royalists were well-trained, well-equipped, and had a strong element of efficient cavalry. It is said that although the Parliamentarian officers were against opposing this force, a group of soldiers went out to scout the enemy positions. They went along the old road to Whalley and in the early morning they lay in hiding along the road side above the old bridge at Read. When a party of Royalists appeared it is said that one of the hiding soldiers accidentally fired his musket, the Royalists retreated in fear of ambush, and as a result the whole of Lord Derby's force withdrew. The Parliamentary forces were thus left with the upper hand in Lancashire. In the year 1643 Nicholas Cunliffe and Robert Cunliffe of Sparth were appointed as sequestrators for confiscating Royalist property. In 1649 they were both appointed to the County Committee which sat monthly at Preston.

The year 1643 brought the war very close to Wycoller when the Duke of Newcastle came down from Skipton to invade Lancashire. The locals had suffered a great deal from the raids of the Skipton Royalists. John Halstead of Swinden Hall in Marsden had his home looted on more than one occasion. In 1643 he recorded, "I had taken from Swinden by the garrison of Skipton 10 oxen and two other beasts to the value of £45 as the market was then, the plunder of my house at their pleasure which I know not how to value". This

52

situation must have occurred in many farms throughout the area. Newcastle's troops arrived in Colne on 30 July 1643. The Parliamentary forces met at "a general rendezvous between both Hundreds in the most remote part of the County upon the borders of Yorkshire to a place called Emmett Lane Head to be a terror to the Yorkshire Cavaliers". The skirmish that followed is thought to have been fought near Colne cemetery.

The following year 1644 Prince Rupert advanced into Lancashire with his cavalry estimated at twenty thousand men. After victory

This painting is supposed to show Christmas festivities at Wycoller Hall in the Stuart period. It was painted in reverse as the artist who had never been to Wycoller copied the background from a reversed engraving. In *Romantic Wycoller* the background is correct but the more observant will note that the figures are reversed and the revelers appear left-handed

Royalist defeat

at Bolton he advanced and occupied Blackburn. Half his force travelled via Clitheroe to Skipton while the other half went by way of Burnley and Colne. It was during this campaign that the Cunliffe's home at Hollins was plundered. Prince Rupert proved to be on his way to defeat at Marston Moor, and soon Parliament had full control of the country. The Cunliffes who had actively supported the Parliamentary cause gained civil appointments in the peace that followed. John Cunliffe and his son Nicholas both became members of the Presbyterian form of church government in Lancashire. In the *History of Marsden and Nelson* Walter Bennett commented, "It is significant that though Burnley could produce three men fit to take part in governing the church in Blackburnshire, only Nicholas Cunliffe of Wycoller could be found in this district fit for such a position". The records of Altham church record, "December 4th 1653, Died Mr Robert Cunliffe. Member of the High Court of Parliament, Justice of the Peace, and member of the Church. He valued himself more on the last account than the other". It is likely that Robert was brother to Nicholas Cunliffe of Wycoller. Little else is known of Nicholas Cunliffe of Wycoller but by 1660 his wife Elizabeth was living alone at Wycoller with her son Ellis.

Poll Tax 1660

The returns for the poll tax levied in 1660 list all the people over the age of sixteen years who were living in Wycoller at that time.

Mrs Elizabeth Cunliffe
Ellis Cunliffe her son
James Hargreaves
James Clegg   her servants
Isabell Cunliffe

James Hartley
Alison his wife
James Atkinson
James Hartley   his servants
Hellen Hartley

Barnard Hartley
Hellen his wife
Christopher
Roger   his sons and daughters
Elizabeth

John Kippax
Alison his wife
Michael Pighles
Eliz Hartley   his servants
Grace Pighles

Robert Emott
John Bentley
Marie Latterke   his servants

James Foulds
Anne his wife
John
James   his sonnes

The families noted below had an income of less than £5 per annum.

Nicholas Cunliffe
Thomasin his wife
Susan Riley   his servant

Roger Hartley
Sarah his wife

John Ambler
Alice his wife
Hellen Smith his servant

Richard Smith
Margarett his wife

John Shaw
Anne his wife
Thomasin Shaw   his servant

James Ambler
Maria his wife
Annes
Thomas
Elizabeth   his four daughters
Marie

Robert Riley
Jennet his wife

55

This Poll Tax list of 1660 gives us an admirable census of Wycoller. If the tax collectors were reliable then here we have a list of everyone over the age of sixteen years who was living in Wycoller at that time. With the help of wills, inventories, and parish registers interesting cameos of Wycoller life in the Stuart period can be gained. Sufficient information to give a full picture has obviously not survived but we are fortunate to get a glimpse of so many Wycoller families of the day.

Cunliffes

We can see from the list that the Cunliffes were still present in the village in two separate families. Elizabeth Cunliffe now a widow was living with her son Ellis and three servants, but the value of her yearly income shows that although she was placed first on the list she was not the wealthiest inhabitant of Wycoller. The other Cunliffe family was that of Nicholas Cunliffe and his wife Thomasin, who are listed as a family with an income of under five pounds a year. Nicholas was probably the son of Nicholas and Elizabeth Cunliffe of Wycoller who was baptised in 1618.

John Kippax

The wealthiest man in Wycoller was John Kippax. It is likely that John Kippax was related to the Kippax family of Schofield farm in Marsden as he moved back to Little Marsden later in his life. In 1656 it was Edward Kippax of Marsden who was the ringleader when a crowd assembled at a Quaker funeral and beat John Sagar of Heyhead as he buried his own child. John Kippax of Wycoller will also be remembered for his inhuman treatment of Quakers.

At the restoration of the monarchy in May 1660 religious persecution was renewed, and the Quakers suffered more than any other denomination. Their different religious practices, their refusal to bear arms and to take oaths made them a target for church and state. They were the smallest of the nonconformist groups, but after the Restoration thousands of them were soon in prison.

It was only six months after the Restoration that John Kippax of Wycoller, then High Constable, learned of a Quaker meeting in Trawden. He took between six and ten soldiers with him and, after first letting the unsuspecting Quakers settle to their meeting, he broke into the farmhouse and, cursing the Friends in a rough manner, encouraged the soldiers to cut and slash them. The full and detailed story is told in the records of the Quakers of Little Marsden. During the same period Quaker records also report: "And from William Kippax of Wycoller husbandman for vs [5s]

1660.

1660/61

Upon y 10th day of y 12th month in y year 1660/61 ffriends being mett together at y house of John Hartley of Gilford Clough, & John Kippac of Wycoler high Constable came into y meeting with half a dozen or ten train band Souldjers with Swords & staves & haled friends forte in a most rude manor, & bade y Souldjers tutt them & flash them & forthwith guarded us to Colne & Comitted us into y Scgool-house, & y day following being y Second day of y week had us before John Starkey of Huntroyd called Justice who tendered us y Oaths of Allegiance & Supremacy & upon our Refusall to Sweare made a mittimus & Comitted us prisoners to y Castle of Lancaster where we remained prisoners most of us Lying upon Straw in a bold high Room till about y 25th of y next month following (about six weeks) & then was Released by Judge Twisden

The Names of friends who were taken from y sd meeting to Lancaster prison are as follows.

Richard Hargreaves of Edgend.   Mary Wilkinson
John Sagar, Stephen Sagar,   Janet Swain
John Hartley, James Smithson   Jane Clayton
John Smith Joseph Cawtree   Alice Hoap.
John Hargreaves, Samuel Driver   Jane Wriglsworth
Richard Mitchell : Willm Whally, Mary Mitchell
Robert Atkinson   Ellen Pollard
Nicholas Whittaker   Anne Pollard
Peter Shackleton Willm Hoap.   Elizabeth Birdie
                                 Anne Parker.

fine ye same officers took two pewter dishes & cloath worth viiijs [9s] & returneth nothing again". It is interesting to speculate that William Kippax the Quaker might well have been a relation of John Kippax the persecutor.

By 1675 John Kippax had moved back to Little Marsden, most probably a return to the family home. In 1675 he leased part of his Wycoller estate to William Lowcock of Salterforth, "for getting and leading away of turves only". In April 1676 "John Kippax of Little Marsden and his wife Allison" finally sold their farm and land in Wycoller to William Lowcock, whose family was to retain it for several generations. John Kippax and his family were remembered for some time in the farm's name Kippax Tenement, however, the name lasted only for a generation or so.

Hartleys   There are three Hartley families in the Wycoller Poll Tax list, those of Barnard Hartley, James Hartley and Roger Hartley. The baptism registers of Colne parish church show that the Hartleys were as prolific as ever. Barnard Hartley had children Roger, Christopher, Elizabeth, Margaret, Isabel, Elizabeth, Barnard, John, Alleson and John, in the sixteen forties and fifties. The second John was baptised after the death of the first but the second John also died in 1659. The 1660 tax list shows only Christopher, Roger and Elizabeth over the age of sixteen and living at home. Barnard Hartley himself died in 1695 and in his will he bequeathed to his grandson Barnard Hartley, "the stone troughs and stone benches that are in and about my new dwelling house in Wycoller."

James Hartley, the head of the second Hartley family, died in 1661 and was buried at Colne on 20 February 1661. His will shows a scrawly attempted signature, probably due to the seriousness of his illness. The witnesses were John Kippax, Barnard Hartley, James Foulds and Robert Smith and their signatures are appended

Signatures of prominent Wycoller inhabitants from the will of James Hartley, 1661 to the will. The inventories of many Stuart wills become more interesting as they frequently list the contents of the house room by room. James had a kitchen, a kitchen chamber, a milk-house, a chamber over the house, a parlour behind the fire, a lower parlour, and the body of the house. James was a substantial yeoman with a large stock of cattle and a hundred sheep. His clothes and purse were valued at £52 and he had debts of over £200 owing to him. The hundred sheep were valued at £17 and we can see that the £200 in debts represents a small fortune for 1661.

In his barn James had, seventeen sacks of oats, harness for horses and hay. He had two waynes and three carts. In the chamber over the house was the weaving equipment as well as a four poster bed and other furnishings. He had "one paire of loomes, healds, spininge wheeles a pair of combes & wooll cards". Beef and bacon to the value of £2 were stored in the parlour behind the fire and not in the kitchen and the lower parlour contained a bed and full bed linen. It appears that the room termed 'the body of the house' was common to all and that most other rooms were used for the dual purpose of bedrooms and storage rooms.

The Poll Tax records Robert Emmott with an income of £20 a year and his two servants. He may well have been a widower with children under sixteen years old who would not be listed on the tax return. The Hearth Tax return of 1666 shows that Robert lived in a substantial house with six hearths, which equalled the Cunliffes, the Kippaxes and the Hartleys. The Emmott family originated at Emmott near Wycoller and from the earliest times members of the family were found in Wycoller. *Emmott family*

It is the Emmott family which gives us a hint that the Poll Tax return may not in fact be a full list of all the inhabitants of Wycoller. James Emmott and his wife had several children in Wycoller from 1640 to 1660. James himself died in 1660 and his wife died in Wycoller in 1662 yet none of them appear on the tax list. George Emmott also lived in Wycoller, where his children were born in this period. George died in Wycoller in 1679 but he does not appear in the list either. The answer could be that poorer families were not listed or that some families were missed by moving in and out of the village.

In October 1669 Anne the wife of James Foulds died. The burial registers at this period are brief and rarely is more detail recorded than the name and date of burial. However, on this occasion the *Village midwife* minister did note the fact that Anne Foulds was a midwife. As village midwife Anne would have played an important part in village life. When we see the list of children born in Wycoller during this period it is likely that Anne Foulds acted as midwife at most of the births. The Foulds family were one of the earliest in Wycoller and branches of the family remained there for several centuries.

Amblers

The Amblers were represented by the families of John and James. Both John and James had incomes below £5 a year and were certainly not among Wycoller's wealthy inhabitants. John had no children over sixteen but we know from the baptisms of his children that in 1660 he had a young family of three children, Elizabeth, Mary and John. James had a family of four daughters, and his wife died in 1669. In July 1674 John Ambler "de Deyne in Wickoller" died and in his will was styled husbandman, certainly a lesser position than yeoman. He had a dozen cattle and twenty sheep as well as a loom and other weaving equipment.

Richard and Margaret Smith were the parents of the first twins recorded in Wycoller. William and Isabel Smith were born in January 1659. Unfortunately William survived only for a few weeks. Robert Riley and his wife Jennet are the only family whose home we can trace. They lived at Height Laithe overlooking Wycoller and they had several children baptised in the sixteen sixties. Jennet died in 1673 but Robert lived until 1709. Little is known about the Shaw family except that they arrived in Wycoller about 1650 and stayed there for several generations.

John Whitaker

Families were coming and going at Wycoller and within ten years of the Poll Tax several important new families had arrived and settled there. John Whitaker was a clothier who came to Wycoller shortly after 1660 and settled in a well-appointed farmhouse. He died in 1671 and his will shows that apart from his dealings in cloth he was a substantial yeoman farmer with cattle, horses and sheep. The inventories of goods were becoming longer now as yeoman families possessed more furniture and personal possessions.

The Fairbank tragedy

The story of the Fairbank family is a tragic one. Michael Fairbank came to farm in Wycoller about the year 1670 and his children Maria and John were born there. In 1681 he died and was buried on 28 February. Only three days later his wife Elizabeth was also buried, and in the second week in March his daughter Maria died.

To open Michael Fairbank's original will and to see the shaky and spidery writing of a man dying of a disease such as smallpox makes one feel a link with the tragedy of the time. Michael's will shows that he had cattle and sheep of considerable value, although careful scrutiny of the debts appended to the inventory shows that these cancel out almost the whole of the family's possessions. The parish registers do not, unfortunately, give the cause of the deaths in the Fairbank family. When Susanah Riley died in Wycoller in 1687 the minister commented that she "dyed of ye pocks". The Fairbank family must also have died of smallpox or some other highly infectious disease.

John Pearson

John Pearson and his family settled in Wycoller and John became a substantial yeoman farmer. As he lived in a three-storied house and his cattle grazed in the fields up to Height Laithe there is little doubt that John Pearson lived at Wycoller Hall. On the ground floor he had a parlour, living room or house, buttery, kitchen and milk-house, and there were seven upstairs rooms which included a chamber over the porch. The rooms were all comfortably furnished and for the first time in Wycoller there is evidence of a house furnished in style and comfort. In the body of the house there was a substantial table and forms, a long settle and six chairs. There was an impressive iron range, with iron racks, spits, dripping pan and other iron gear. This was the old fireplace at Wycoller Hall not the mock antique fire-place built by Henry Owen Cunliffe a century later. There was a spice cupboard probably let into the wall and a salt chest. Against the wall was an item that John Pearson was probably proud of—and one that few other Wycoller families possessed—a long case clock.

(Right) The south end of Wycoller Hall

(Below Spice cupboard at Laithe Hills Cottage

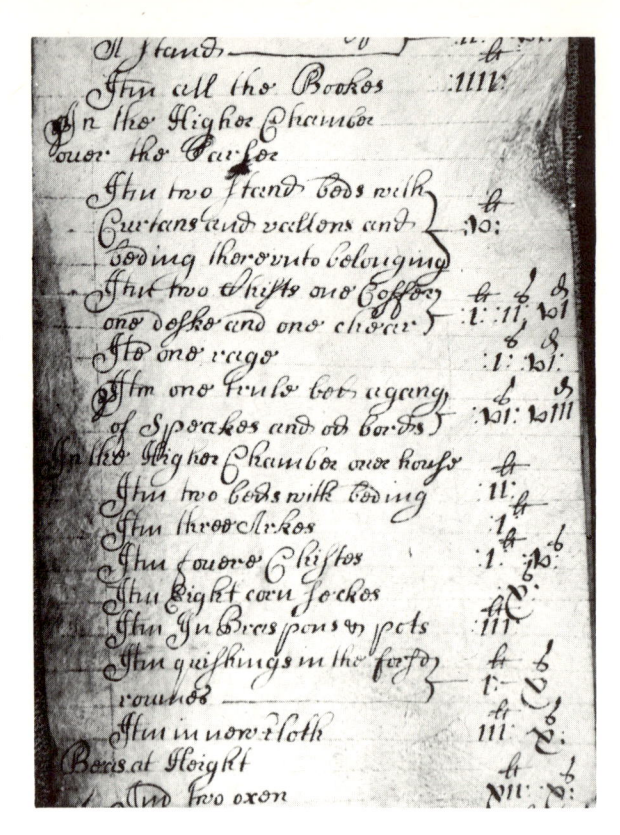

Part of the inventory of John Pearson who died in 1695

Somewhere there had to be a loom and John kept his in the kitchen along with the meal ark and the store of beef and bacon. There were some attractive upstairs rooms in his house. In the chamber over the parlour there was "one stand bed Curtains and vallons and beding thereunto belonging, one range, one Chist, one little table with a carpet, a little Cobert, and four Chears". In the chamber over the milk-house there was a stand bed with curtains and fittings, a cupboard, two boxes, a little trunk and a looking glass. The house had plenty of linen, pewter and silver plate, and the rooms were furnished with a wide variety of furniture including chests, desks, cupboards, chairs and stools. John Pearson died in 1695 and over a yard of parchment was needed to list the contents of his house room by room. His son John Pearson inherited, and the Pearson family remained in Wycoller for several generations later giving their name to Pearson's Farm.

62

Thomas Eyre's Account

Our first real insight into Wycoller Hall and the Cunliffe family who lived there comes from Thomas Eyre of Sheffield, who left a scanty but fascinating account of his Cunliffe relations and his visits to Wycoller in the eighteenth century. Thomas Eyre has long been overlooked in the Wycoller story and does not appear on any printed pedigree. His mother, Elizabeth Cunliffe, was sister of Henry Cunliffe of Wycoller. She married John Scargill by whom she had a daughter Sarah; but after his untimely death she married Thomas Eyre of Sheffield and had a further family of whom Thomas Eyre, the subject of our story, was the eldest son.

Thomas was born in King Street, Sheffield, on 23 April 1735 and was apprenticed at an early age to Joseph Owen a Sheffield cutler. The Owens were his relations, for his step-sister, Sarah Scargill, had married Joseph Owen and the family were all engaged in the cutlery business. At this point a family tree is necessary to make the relationships clear. John Cunliffe who stands at the head of the tree was said to be "of Wycoller" in some printed pedigrees. His grandson, Thomas Eyre, tells us otherwise.

> *My grandfather, Mr John Cunliffe, lived at a place called the Hollins, near the village of Accrington. He came to Barnsley in Yorkshire, where he lived as a clerk with Mr Wood, who was a Councellor and J.P. After some time he married Dorothy a daughter of the above Mr Wood by a first marriage . . . His second son, Henry Cunliffe, was baptized at Barnsley and his daughter Elizabeth, who was my mother, was baptized ——— , as appears by the Church Registers in Barnsley. I could find no more in the Register there. But I found his first child, Nicholas was baptized at Accrington; his two other children at Leeds in Yorkshire, viz, William and Anne. He lived some time in Barnsley after his marriage. I have been shown the house he lived in by an old person that knew him. How long he might stay in Barnsley I could not find; but he lived in Leeds (after he left Barnsley) many years, and I suppose died there, but I have not yet learned where he was buried or when. Some time before he died his wife and he were parted, and they never lived together again . . . I never heard of more children that he had than three sons and two daughters (Nicholas, Henry, William, Elizabeth, and Anne)*

It will be noted that Thomas Eyre does not mention that his grandfather, John Cunliffe, ever lived at Wycoller and he probably never did. He died at Leeds in December 1717 aged forty seven.

John Cunliffe of Hollins, Barnsley, and Leeds.
m. Dorothy Wood
d. 18 Dec. 1717 aged 47

Nicholas Cunliffe of Hollins	Henry Cunliffe b. March 1693 1m. Anne Morville 2m. Mary Topham d. 26 June 1773 aged 80.	William Cunliffe of Leeds m. Joan Pickersgill	Elizabeth Cunliffe 1m. John Scargill 2m. Thomas Eyre d. 20 June 1756	Anne Cunliffe
N.I.	N.I.	N.I.		

Sarah (Sally) Scargill m. Joseph Owen d. 2 Jan 1746	Elizabeth (Betty) Eyre m. Webster	Thomas Eyre b. 23 April 1735 m. Sarah Heathcoat 1 May 1766

Henry Owen (alias Henry Owen Cunliffe) m. Mary Oldham 13 Aug 1775 d. 8 Nov 1818 aged 66 N.I.	Charles Owen (alias Charles Cunliffe Owen)	John Webster d. 24 May 1751 at Wycoller Hall

Catherine Eyre b. 1767	Mary Eyre b. 1768	Elizabeth Eyre b. 1770	Thomas Eyre	Joseph Eyre b. 1775	Others

John Cunliffe's eldest son Nicholas was baptised at Accrington and inherited the Wycoller estate after his father's death. It was he who sold Hollins in the year 1723 and thus limited the Cunliffe estates to Wycoller. When he died shortly afterwards his brother Henry inherited Wycoller Hall and estate. Henry Cunliffe, born in Barnsley, went to live in Liverpool, and when he married at Colne Parish Church in May 1721 he was entered as "Henry Cunliffe of Liverpool". Henry's wife Anne was the daughter of Walter Morville of Waterside in Colne and she brought a moderate fortune to the family as her father owned considerable land in Colne.

Thomas Eyre says that his grandfather had intended Henry to study law but that the young Henry left home and joined his relative Foster Cunliffe who was a successful merchant in Liverpool. His father appealed to him to come home again but Henry announced his intention of going to sea. Thomas writes, "My grandfather sent him some money and goods as a venture, when he went on board ship as supercargo. I think my uncle told me he sailed to Guinea; from whence to Maryland; so back to Liverpool. I never heard that he went to sea any more". In view of this comment by his nephew it is interesting to note that Henry is described on most Cunliffe pedigrees as a sea captain.

Thomas Eyre first visited his uncle at Wycoller Hall in the summer of 1744. He rode there on horseback from Sheffield accompanied by his step-sister Sally, Sarah Scargill, and from there we follow his story.

> *I remember the first question he asked me was 'whether I had got the Pope in my belly'. I thought him an odd man. We staid at Wycoller Hall about three weeks, when my uncle having displeased my sister Sally she would go home again; and I being a boy, and ordered by my mother to obey my sister while there, I must go home too. I remember my uncle pressed very hard for us to stay longer, and followed us when we were on horseback up his ground for that purpose, but sister would not stay, which vexed him so much that he said we should not come any more. However, I rode before her home. I must not omit mention of our coming back by way of Leeds, where we stayed two or three days, and called to see Aunt Lumley. She was my uncle William Cunliffe's widow, and had married again to Mr Lumley attorney of Leeds. We drank tea there, I remember; she looked thin, and seemingly very tender.*

Artist's impression of Wycoller Hall in Thomas Eyre's day

Henry Cunliffe's brother William married Joan Pickersgill, daughter of a Leeds tobacconist, but he died without issue. As Thomas Eyre explained, Joan Cunliffe became his Aunt Lumley. Without any children himself and knowing that both his brothers had died childless, Henry Cunliffe was concerned about the future of the Cunliffe family and his Wycoller estate. The position worsened when his wife died in December 1750. Thomas Eyre states "My uncle, Henry Cunliffe, then took a little boy of my sister Webster's, and probably had the boy lived and pleased him would have made him his heir; but he died soon after he got there". The burial records of Colne Parish Church record the burial of John Webster of Wycoller on 24 May 1751. The burial register entries of Anne Cunliffe and John Webster strongly confirm the reliability of Thomas Eyre's account. His story where it can be checked with other sources is usually proved most reliable.

For a time Henry Cunliffe lived alone at Wycoller Hall with his two servants although from time to time his niece Elizabeth Webster and other relations came to stay with him for lengthy visits. It was during this period that Thomas Eyre made his second visit to Wycoller.

> *I do not remember that I went any more to Wycoller, till about the year 1750 or 1751. When I got there my uncle was at Blackpool he being then a widower. I found my sister Webster lived with him. She was glad to see me, and promised to use her interest with my uncle when he came back, as he was displeased at my going to Sheffield with my sister Sally before. The night after I got there my uncle came home. I kept out of his sight till she had let him know that I was come, which he no sooner heard than he flew into a passion, and said I should have stayed before. In justice to my sister Eliza, I must say she pleaded hard for me, saying I was but a child and ordered by my mother to obey Sally. After some time he inquired where I was. She called me to come, and in a few minutes I was great friends again. I stayed a month or six weeks, and it was with some ado that I could get away from him to come home, though I was apprentice to brother Owen; and old Mr Owen was so vexed at my stay in Lancashire, supposing it so much against their son's (my master's) interest, that they would have had him to advertise me as a Runaway, but he did not. My uncle at this time was much bent on marrying some young woman, as he had much increased his estate and he wanted an heir to it. My sister Betty soon after I came home displeased him. My sister Sally was in the same case by coming out of Scotland against his will; and I was a Papist, as he called me, for he was most rigidly prejudiced against Catholics of any one I ever knew. He had a good opinion of me but on that account, for he thought if I got his estate the Priests would have it after me, and Priests he hated. So he married Mary, daughter of Mr Lupton Topham, of Bradley, near Skipton, with a small fortune. She was a very decent, good-looking woman, and likely to have children, being then about —— years of age. He married her about the year 1752.*

Luck seemed to be against the Cunliffe family; not only had Henry's brothers died childless but Henry himself still had no

A chest said to have come from Wycoller Hall

This seventeenth century chair from Wycoller Hall is now in Towneley Hall at Burnley

children even several years after his second marriage. The choice of an heir from his near relations was also certain to prove far from easy. It was in these circumstances that Henry invited Thomas Eyre to Wycoller Hall.

Some years passed, and there being no likelihood of his having children, he sent for me to come to see him (about the year 1756) *I was then about* 21 *years old. My father and brother Owen had been over together about six months before. I no sooner got there than I found a great change in the house, it being kept a great deal cleaner, and better living than before, and something more in furniture. They both made me very welcome. I had been only a few days there before my aunt's sister [Anne Topham] came over on a visit. I found it was a scheme of theirs to make a match betwixt her and me. My uncle and aunt took care to leave us together the first night after she came. In a few days I found she would gladly have married me, but then I must become a Protestant. But I was determined not to become an apostate if I lost his estate and it. I omitted taking notice that my mother died in June* 1756, *and in a letter to my Uncle, acquainting him of it, but in such terms that it was endeavouring to make him believe she was exceedingly ill-treated in her last illness by my Father, or me, or both of us. But he paid no regard to what they wrote: only this, he gave me the letter when I went over the winter after she died, and said, "See Tom, what friends thou hast."*

But to return; my uncle had a notion that he would change my Religion. But my Father being very subject to gout, he thought he would not live long, so would not have me disoblige him, but continue as I was till he dyed. But my Father, after he retired from the "Swan", became more hearty; and I turned of 21 years he expected me to change my religion almost directly. He told me that Mr Topham wanted to make a match betwixt his daughter Anne and me; "and" says he, "he wants me to back it." I told him I would have no objections, but would not meddle in it. "So Tom," says he," you have nothing more to do than knock of your foolish religion, and the job is done. She will be a handsome fortune. Her father is rich and has only one son, who has married Mr. Newby's daughter, of Kilwick, against his father's will, so that he threatened to disinherit him; and she has an uncle in the North very rich who has no children, and she is in great favour with him, so I would advise you to have her; but do not appear to be over forward, or take notice to them of what I say to you." Discourses of this kind often passed between him and me. I was invited over to her Father's who behaved well to me. I stayed a month and then came to Sheffield.

On one occasion there was more than a hint of scandal at Wycoller Hall and Thomas Eyre found himself involved in it. Thomas had never liked his uncle's first wife, his aunt Anne, and described her as "a plain ignorant woman, remarkable for drinking strong tea without sugar". After his uncle's second marriage he found Wycoller Hall a changed place, far cleaner and with better furnishings, and as he got on well with his aunt Mary he found it difficult to listen to scandal against her. It must be remembered that Mary Cunliffe was around thirty years her husband's junior. However, it appears to have been a family affair and none too serious. It is best that we should hear the story first hand.

In three or four months my uncle wrote a letter inviting me over; but as he expected he should not be at home when I got there, he to my astonishment charged me not to take notice of my Aunt or her

A view of Wycoller very much as Thomas Eyre knew it

Sister, or any of her family, for reasons he would tell me when he came back. This confounded me; I did not know how to behave as he directed, as my Aunt on all occasions used me so well. However, I went over, and found no one but my aunt at home. My uncle came at night, then took me on one side and showed me a letter which Katty at the "Hole-in-the-Wall" in Colne had given to him. Katty told him a carrier had given it to her for him. My uncle asked me whether it was Sally's writing. I told him I thought not. He said if he thought it was he would play the devil with her. The letter contained severe reflections on my Aunt, asserting that she had been over free with a relation named Hall, who lived as a servant with my uncle. Which letter Mrs Scargill told me today that my sister Webster told her that she had wrote, and that at the persuasion of my sister Owen. Indeed I never saw any unseemly conduct of that kind in my life, though it has been told I have.

In June 1756 Thomas Eyre's mother, Elizabeth Eyre, née Cunliffe, died aged sixty-one years and was buried in Trinity Churchyard at Sheffield. Thomas Eyre's connections with the Cunliffes and Owens became strained in the years that followed. In 1759 he left employment with the Owen family and took employment with Joseph Wildsmith of Sheffield, still working in the cutlery trade. In May 1766 Thomas Eyre married. He had long since lost contact with the rich and desirable Anne Topham and married Sarah Heathcoat a local Sheffield girl. Thomas would not renounce his religion and married a girl of his own choice rather than a far wealthier girl introduced to him for family reasons. It appears that from that time he had little if any contact with his uncle at Wycoller Hall. His first child, a daughter Catherine, was born in 1767 and from that time he had many children, naming his first son Thomas.

Thomas Eyre began committing his story to paper in June 1780 at the age of forty-five years. He stated briefly, "I have written this account not only for my own satisfaction, but in order to satisfy my children hereafter, that they may not have wrong notions regarding these matters".

Henry Cunliffe, the last Cunliffe of Wycoller, died in June 1773 and was buried in the churchyard at Colne Parish Church on the 24th of the month as shown by a simple entry in the register. Thomas Eyre was remembered in his uncle's will—Henry Cunliffe bequeathed his nephew one shilling!

Henry had made his will in 1769, four years before his death. He stipulated that he was "to be buried in Decent Manner with assistance only of six relations to which I gives Gloves and Hatbands and with the assistance of my tenants to each of whom I give one shilling apiece whose Rents Exceeds not the yearly Rent of Four Pounds". After all the small bequests and provision for his wife Mary, the sole beneficiary was Henry Owen his great-nephew from Sheffield. Money from rents was to be deposited at interest with the Bank of England until he attained the age of twenty-one. The bequest of all his estates to Henry Owen was on condition that "he is now and always hereafter and his Succeeding Heirs take upon himselfe and themsleves the Surname of Cunliffe".

The Last Squire

Baron Cunliffe upon his return from Sheffield brought me a nice apple knife, a neat pair of scissors and an elegant paper Mache snuff box, also a pair of scissors for Nancy Nutter, also another pair for Mary Driver—paid him for all and in all.
Elizabeth Shackleton, Sunday 4 December 1774.

Henry Owen was born in Sheffield in 1752, the son of Joseph Owen of that city. In his younger days his links with Wycoller were tenuous as his mother Sarah was frequently out of favour with her uncle, Henry Cunliffe, the squire at Wycoller Hall. However, Henry Owen was finally chosen by Henry Ciunliffe to be the next squire at Wycoller on condition that he took the name of Cunliffe. Henry Cunliffe assisted Henry Owen's education at Bolton Abbey School and at Oxford University. In his will Henry Cunliffe stipulated that his great-nephew Henry should study law at the Inns of Court, until he attained the age of twenty four. He did not study law, however, but went to Oxford university. It is unlikely that he completed his studies as he came to Wycoller immediately on the death of his great-uncle in June 1773.

Henry Owen Cunliffe arrived at Wycoller in late June and soon made contact with other local families. On Friday 9 July Elizabeth Shackleton of Alkincoats, noted in her diary, "Tom went for the first time to pay a morning's visit to the young Squire at Wycoller Mr Cunliffe". The Shackletons had known old Henry Cunliffe and were among the first to make contact with the new squire. Elizabeth Shackleton's sons Tom and John were soon good friends with Henry and he dined with the family at Alkincoats on 11 July. On the 14th the young men all went shooting together and Henry came back with them and stayed the night at Alkincoats. When he returned to Wycoller the next day the three Shackleton sons John, Tom and Robin returned with him to dine there. The friendship developed quickly; they met on the 9th, dined together on the 14th and on the 17th got drunk together.

Elizabeth Shackleton tells us that her husband and two sons accompanied Henry to Pendle Hill and that on the excursion they met two other gentlemen friends and celebrated together. The party seems to have split up, for Elizabeth records that her husband arrived home at 1 a.m. but sons Tom and John did not arrive until 2 a.m. The revelry ended a day or so later when Henry's mother and sister arrived to stay with him at Wycoller.

Elizabeth Shackleton Much of the information about Henry Owen Cunliffe has come from the diaries of Elizabeth Shackleton. Elizabeth, the only daughter of John Parker of Browsholme, was born 16 December 1726. At the age of twenty years she married her second cousin, Robert Parker of Alkincoats, and by him she had three sons Thomas, John and Robert. Her husband died in 1759 and six years later in 1765 she married John Shackleton a local wool dealer who was nearly twenty years her junior. After her eldest son Thomas came of age in December 1776 he took up residence at Alkincoats and in 1777 the Shackletons moved to the newly built Pasture House at Barrowford.

One of the main entertainments of the local gentry was the social round of wining and dining with neighbours. Henry enjoyed this immensely. In August 1774 he joined the Shackletons at Alkincoats to dine on a haunch of venison which had been sent from Browsholme, Elizabeth Shackleton's former home and one of the few country houses still retaining a herd of deer at that time. Henry had a small dinner party to meet the Emmotts of Emmott Hall and in his turn was invited to hunt with them and dine at Emmott. To visit Wycoller was no easy journey for the Shackletons and Elizabeth often bemoaned the bad roads. In September 1773 Elizabeth and her husband were returning from dining at Wycoller Hall when they suffered an accident: "At Bough Gap a cow in the lane near that house turned her backside broke the glass in 100 pieces and the Pannel of the chaise door on John's side—a bad accident—shocking roads".

On one occasion in January 1777 Thomas Clayton of Carr Hall in Barrowford and Henry Owen Cunliffe organised a dance at the Red Lion in Colne. Elizabeth wrote to Thomas Clayton declining his invitation and noted in her diary, "I answered to Mr T. Clayton, told him the smallpox was so general I had not for months, nor did not stir from home". The Waltons of Marsden Hall were also very much involved in the social round and Henry dined there many times. On Saturday 22 August 1778 he went there along with the Shackletons to dine on a haunch of venison from Towneley. Elizabeth was not impressed on that occasion: "The haunch of

Extract from the diary of Elizabeth Shackleton, 26 December, 1778, written inside the front cover

venison so tender it tasted rotten it was short of roasting a full hour, the Prunes not good, Peaches nectarines shocking. Plumbs and Pears excellent". On another occasion when Henry had dined at Marsden Hall he enthused to Elizabeth that "he had pineapple and melon, cherries and three sorts of grapes".

The finest banquets took place at Christmas time, and on Saturday 26 December 1778 Elizabeth Shackleton prepared a great feast at Pasture House. "Great cooking and preparation for Company to dine: my son's Feast Day... Dined here this day Mr Thos Clayton Messrs Cunliffe, Bulcock, Ecroyd, Whitaker, Hartley, Shaw, Burton, Metcalf. The dinner well got. A fine turkey, apple dumplings, roast beef, marrow bones, Ham, 2 fine fowles, little mutton pies, Veal collops, a noble duck, mince pies, sausages, Potted Head... all went peaceably the Bishop of Colne the most done for, broke several glasses and a plate, would go home did so. Whitaker riotous to a degree. Burton drunk Cunliffe moralizing. Shackleton sulky quarrelsome—sleepy all ended well".

Wycoller Hall Feast

That same evening when everyone was full of turkey, roast beef, mince pies and port Henry issued invitations for a feast at Wycoller Hall. But Henry was unlucky, the day of the Wycoller feast was "a wet windy day". The rain turned the rough roads to Wycoller into muddy streams and Elizabeth records, "not a creature at Wycoller yesterday but Messrs Whitaker, Parker and Shackleton two o'clock when they got home. Mr. Shackleton wet to the skin". Poor Henry, his feasts at Wycoller never had the appeal of Marsden Hall or Carr Hall even without the weather being against him.

Henry was not very impressed with the "yeoman" type hall that had satisfied his predecessors. As a middle-class tradesman's son pulled into the lesser gentry he aspired to a hall fit for the rôle he intended to play. He had visited the Waltons at Marsden Hall, the Claytons at Carr Hall and the Parkers at Alkincoats and he wished to have a home to rival theirs. Henry wished to marry and knew that he would have to make an attractive residence to draw a desirable bride to Wycoller. He made his plans for the Hall and moved out from Wycoller to let the builders get on with the work. On Saturday 5 February 1774 "Cunliffe left Wycoller and housekeeping and went with his men and horses to the Red Lyon". For well over a year he made the Red Lion in Colne his home. The easy access to ale and wine was one benefit for the inconvenience for Henry loved his wine. When wine deliveries arrived in Colne the largest barrel was sure to be his.

Courtship

"It is a truth universally acknowledged that a single man in possession of a good fortune must be in want of a wife". So Jane Austen opened her novel *Pride and Prejudice*, and our story at Wycoller has much in common with Jane's plots. Although Henry had no great fortune he was certainly the area's eligible bachelor. However, he had no wish to be a catch for some local lady. If there was going to be any catching Henry was going to do it. In 1773 he was thwarted in an attempt to court Miss Wilcox of Thornton. In 1774 Elizabeth Shackleton noted that he "set out for Sheffield to see the rich and beautiful Miss Smith". There is no doubt that Henry had his sights set high, for in July he boasted that he could have a "fortune by a lady of £9,000" but thought that he deserved "three times that sum".

Mary Oldham

In May 1775 Henry went to Manchester on his Militia exercises taking a servant with him. When he returned a month later, Elizabeth noted that he was "In spirits about the youngest Miss Oldham of Manchester". How and when Henry met Mary we do not know for certain but it is highly likely that it was while in Manchester on his Militia training. Perhaps the romantic meeting had taken place at some ball that he had attended with his fellow officers. Whatever the case, he seems to have been truly smitten and fallen in love with both Mary and her financial prospects.

Marriage

Mary was the daughter of Adam Oldham a wealthy hat manufacturer of Manchester, and the marriage was arranged for August 1775. Mary's father Adam must have given his blessing to the marriage, but was he happy at his daughter's choice? In one respect the wealthy tradesman's daughter had caught the squire, yet to quote Jane Austen: "A poor honourable is no catch, and I cannot imagine any liking in the case, for, take away his rents, and the poor baron has nothing. What a difference a vowel makes! If his rents were equal to his rants!"

On Tuesday 8 August 1775 Henry left Colne to travel to Manchester for his wedding. The ceremony took place on the 13th at the "Collegiate and Parish Church of Manchester," now Manchester Cathedral. The marriage certificate can be seen in the Cathedral registers with the details. "Henry Owen Cunliffe of the Chapelry of Colne Esq., and Mary Oldham of the parish and town of Manchester Spinster". After the wedding the couple set out for a honeymoon in London accompanied by Mary's sister Hannah.

Renovations

Meanwhile back at Wycoller extensive rebuilding work was being done at the Hall. The work that had begun in February 1774 was only just completed by July the following year. The time factor alone is a guide to the amount of work that was done on both interior and exterior. A porch with ornate finials was added to the Hall, a new range of high mullioned windows was placed in the west wall, and a large ancient-style fire-place was constructed. The three-storied end of the Hall had new windows fitted, including a fine venetian window, and the interiors were modernised. For the first time the farm-like surroundings of the Hall were laid out as gardens and new trees were planted.

From time to time Henry visited Wycoller to keep an eye on developments and once his wedding day was settled it became imperative that the Hall should be ready for his return to Wycoller

The eighteenth century porch from Wycoller Hall as it stood for many years in Trawden

A romantic impression of Wycoller Hall in the late eighteenth century

A more realistic drawing of Wycoller Hall entitled "Wycoller Hall in 1819"

with his bride. Elizabeth Shackleton twice went to see the alterations at Wycoller. The first occasion was on Friday 28 July 1775 when she was accompanied by Henry and a few friends. She noted "great improvements indeed. Mrs Pearson invited us all to drink tea". What a great pity she did not say any more, not a word about the new porch, only that they had tea at Mrs. Pearson's. Her second visit was in August while Henry was away and she says little about the visit except that she "reconoitred Cunliffes House, it rained, but a nice out".

The Cunliffes did not return to take up residence at Wycoller Hall until Monday 4 December. "Mr and Mrs Cunliffe in the Chaise Hugh the driver, came to take up their abode for the first time at Wycoller." On the last Sunday in December they made their first appearance together for morning service at Colne Parish Church.

The Baron

Henry Owen Cunliffe was known locally as "the Baron" or "Baron Cunliffe," the nickname being given in recognition of his ambitious life style and in mockery of his small stature and pompous manner. Elizabeth frequently refers to him as Baron Cunliffe and also as Learned Cunliffe, probably a sarcastic reference to his Oxford education. A few of Elizabeth's diary entries illustrate the case.

Monday 4 July 1774.   "At ten at night the Learned Cunliffe came from London from Preston to Wycoller to examine his house".

Sunday 10 July 1774.   "The Great Cunliffe at Church".

Wednesday 19 October 1774.   "Tom and Mr. Shackleton dined with Baron Cunliffe at his dormitory at the Red Lyon, Colne".

Friday 14 August 1778.   "Tom shot a brace himself. He and Mr Shackleton had an invitation from the Baron to his mansion—they went".

14 March 1781   "Yesterday the Baron & his lady of the Dale went to make a wedding visit to Mr & Mrs Wainman at Carr Head".

A Sporting life

Without a doubt Henry was a keen sportsman. He enjoyed hunting, shooting, fishing, and cock-fighting—in fact all the sports both active and passive that were available in the eighteenth century for a north country squire to indulge in. When he first arrived at Wycoller he was young and above all he enjoyed riding and hunting. In his first few weeks as a young squire at Wycoller Henry went hunting with the Parkers, the Emmotts of Emmott and the Waltons. He hunted in Winewall, round Pendle, in Craven, at Bradford and at Wigan. Henry enjoyed both the pomp of the hunt and the thrill of the chase. On Friday 18 March 1774 "Baron Cunliffe, his valet, groom and hunters all in parade and high pomp set out for the Wigan Hunt". On Sunday 7 February 1779 John Parker enjoyed a "capital fox chase at Bradford where Cunliffe upon his little horse beat all the hunt". Henry also enjoyed attendance at race meetings as well as riding himself and was seen at races in both Lancashire and Yorkshire. Henry's next preferences to hunting were shooting and fishing. He often went shooting with the Parkers and Emmotts and occasionally with the Waltons. On several occasions they dined on Boulsworth Hill during their shooting excursions. Often he delivered grouse, pheasants and rabbits to the Shackleton household. Whitewell was one of his customary fishing resorts.

When Henry moved to Yorkshire after the turn of the century he was about fifty years old. From this period his sporting activities slowed down and took a change from active sports to more passive spectator sports. Tradition has it that the sport that took the squire's fancy above all others was the bloody sport of cock-fighting. There is evidence that Henry visited bull baiting performances at Laneshawbridge, but there is only slight evidence of his cock-fighting activities. Nevertheless it is very likely true, as the local gentry were usually the leaders in this sport which at that time was considered a noble one. The first written link between Henry and cock-fighting comes from Mrs Gaskell in *The Life of Charlotte Brontë*. Although he is not mentioned by name it became fairly obvious that the reference is to Henry Owen Cunliffe.

Cock-fighting

> *Another Squire, of a more distinguished family and larger property—one is then led to imagine of better education but that does not always follow—died at his house, not many miles from Haworth, only a few years ago. His great amusement and occupation had been cock-fighting. When he was confined to his chamber with what he knew would be his last illness, he had his cocks brought up there, and watched the bloody battle from his bed. As his mortal disease increased, and it became impossible for him to turn so as to follow the combat, he had looking glasses arranged in such a*

81

"The Ruling Passion" by Lanslett John Pott, R.A.

manner, around and above him, as he lay, that he could still see the cocks fighting, And in this manner he died.

There is an interesting painting by Lanslett John Pott, R.A., portraying an eighteenth century gentleman and his friends holding a cock-fighting meeting indoors. This painting, "The Ruling Passion" is popularly associated with Squire Cunliffe and Wycoller Hall. Pott was not painting until half a century after the death of Squire Cunliffe but he could well have read the story from Mrs Gaskell. A second picture in the same style, "Game to the Last" portrays a gentleman reclining ill in bed while a cock fight is held on the carpet. These paintings could well relate to Lord Derby who was also reported to have been so keen on cock-fighting that he would hold cock fights on his counterpane when he was ill in bed. The backgrounds of the paintings with high ceilings, oil paintings, classical vases and coloured servants are hardly in keeping with Wycoller Hall.

A depression above the old gardens at Wycoller Hall is said to have been a cock-pit

Captain Cunliffe

Henry Owen Cunliffe served in the Militia both in Lancashire and Yorkshire. He joined the Lancashire Militia soon after coming to Wycoller but Elizabeth Shackleton was certainly unimpressed by his military presence. On Sunday 24 July 1774 she tells us, "Went to Church by myself—Cunliffe in his Regimentals of the Royal Lancashires—a little Captain. I knew that Cunliffe was at Church this day in his Regimentals a small Captain—no honour to the Royal Lancashires. Brought his new whisky to Coln, his new man in his elegant new livery, red hair well powdered, two new hunters . . . . Cunliffe is too short, too low—wants inches for a captain, a Petit, trop Petit Captain". When Henry moved into Yorkshire he was gazetted in February 1809 as Captain in the Craven Regiment of Local Militia.

Henry had his troubles from time to time when personal relationships broke down. In February 1778 he upset Elizabeth Shackleton for some reason or other and she was not willing to see him. However, she went to visit her son and met Henry there. "At 9 at night as supper was going into the parlour, Cunliffe came in, I called him a low life rascal—said I wondered he had the impudence to come where I was, said I would spit in his face—my nephew to blame to ask him to come here and had got me here".

By the end of the month Elizabeth was still complaining about Henry but there is a hope of reconciliation "a few very disagreeable sharp feeling words about Cunliffe—time I hope will wear all off—and true friendship ever subside amongst us all for ever". By August

1778 Elizabeth noted, "Tom sent a large basket of gooseberries a present to the family at Wycoller Hall, wish they may part sober in peace and friendship—All our guests returned safely from the Wycoller Rant. No quarrelling all Peace".

In March of the same year Henry had a serious argument in Colne. The day was Monday 6 April: "Squire Cunliffe and Squire Higgin this noon at Coln Cross had a smart engagement. Squire Higgin sent a greyhound to be kept at Wycoller and Cunliffe said it should not be there. Cunliffe spit in Higgin's face. He returned the compliment to Cunliffe. Cunliffe gave Higgin a blow which Higgin returned and a Pritty Battle ensued. When over, Cunliffe remounted his Rosenanta and followed the carriage which contained his amiable lady and the beautiful Miss Oldham who were proceeding to Manchester where Mrs Cunliffe is to remain for some time."

Henry was not one to hold his tongue when he felt that something had to be said, and more than occasionally he insulted people. On Monday 5 December 1774 Elizabeth tells us, "Cunliffe, last Thurs at the White Horse meeting, very rude to Dr Midgely, told him his daughter was a whore, and common to all—very polite behaviour, generous and like the Oxonian that professes the Gentleman". Henry must have had a serious dispute with Dr Midgely for a fortnight later when he visited the Shackletons, Elizabeth noted, "Cunliffe came to supper and to stay all night he did not. A great conversation about the dispute betwixt him and Dr Midgely—Cunliffe very high indeed".

Henry occasionally came off the worst in his arguments as Elizabeth records in September 1778: "Jack Shaw and Cunliffe went a setting got one brace, Jack the conqueror, princely pastime sought".

The following day Elizabeth tells us that her son John went to Wycoller to dine with Henry and she reported. "Mr Tom Clayton to dine there—Cunliffe can't appear, Jack Shaw's fist has left considerable black marks on his face".

An interesting insight into the occupants of Wycoller Hall is given on Tuesday 29 December 1778 when Elizabeth records. "Cunliffe called at Alkincoats for a medicine for himself wife 2 maids 1 man two boys his little Horse five dogs—occasioned by a favourite dog of Mrs Cunliffe's going mad all the family to take it tomorrow morning all went very merry before tea". The Parkers of Alkincoats were owners of the prescription of a renowned medicine for the

84

These stone gate posts near Height Laithe mark the entrance to the coach road that leads to Wycoller Hall

treatment of hydrophobia in humans and animals. This prescription had belonged to William Hill of Ormskirk, at one time concerned in the affairs of Alkincoats Hall, who had bequeathed it by will to the Parkers. People came from distances of forty or fifty miles to take the medicine. Elizabeth's record on the occasion of Henry's visit to take the medicine gives us a census return of the Hall for 1778 down to the last dog.

In December 1778 Elizabeth noted that: "Matthew Oddie drank tea here came to shew me the plan he had executed for Mr Cunliffe, neat indeed". The plan referred to was an estate map. Plans of several Colne estates surveyed by Matthew Oddie have survived but that of the Wycoller estate of Henry Owen Cunliffe has not been traced.

We have seen that Elizabeth Shackleton frequently refers to Henry with sarcasm and criticism. Yet she gives him a regular mention in her diary and certainly took a great interest in his activities. The Cunliffes were also welcome guests and dined regularly with the Shackletons. When together with the Waltons they dined at Pasture House in 1778 Elizabeth commented, "Mrs Cunliffe a great talker, high head, and her hair very rough a queer pair and uncouth". On another occasion when she visited her son at Alkincoats she noted: "Mr Cunliffe was the Headmaster of ceremonies, his lady there and they drank tea at night, then played the half crown whist, the Baroness of the Vale called it a good family game—they supped at ten—set off for home past twelve—they had a great deal of small talk—quite heathens".

Henry thought of leaving Wycoller several times. In November 1778 he talked to his friends of leasing Ackworth Park near Pontefract for twenty years and later he came close to taking a house at Addingham. Eventually, in 1802 he did lease Chapel House in Wharfedale and lived there for several years returning to Wycoller only once or twice a year to collect his rents and to shoot grouse. Henry finally returned to Wycoller and died at Wycoller Hall on 8 November 1818. He was buried in St Bartholomew's, the Parish Church in Colne, where a brass plaque can still be found on a step in the chancel.

Death of Henry Owen Cunliffe

Here lies the body of
Henry Owen Cunliffe
of Wycoller Hall. Died
8 Nov., 1818. Aged 66.

Henry made his last will and testament in August 1807 making his nephew, Charles Cunliffe Owen, his heir at law. The executors were Thomas Clayton of Carr Hall and Thomas Parker of Alkincoats, and his wife Mary. However, Thomas Parker died before any action had been taken on the will, and Thomas Clayton and Mary Cunliffe renounced their executorship. The position was very complex as most of the property and lands had been heavily mortgaged. In the early days Henry had increased his Wycoller estate: he had added Parson Lee as early as September 1773, buying the farm for £980.

(Above) Henry Owen Cunliffe's Hall soon fell into ruins—adjoining cottages survived longer

(Left) The Cunliffe Hatchment in Colne Parish Church

However, during the following forty years Henry had mortgaged and borrowed far more than he could repay. Frequently when foreclosure was threatened he had to borrow from a second source to pay the first. John Stonehouse, who had a £3,000 mortgage on some Cunliffe property claimed that he had loaned Henry a further £1,500 without security.

During the nineteenth century the Cunliffe estate became split up between the mortgagees and farms were sold at various times by order of the Court of Chancery. For many years the main part of the estate was in the possession of John Oldham the only son of Hannah Oldham, sister of Henry Owen Cunliffe's wife Mary, and later it passed to the Rev. John Roberts Oldham.

In May 1858 James Hartley, yeoman of Wycoller, died and left farms, land and cottages to his son Richard Hartley. Richard also purchased the farms and cottages in Wycoller which had been held by the Rev. John Roberts Oldham. At a further sale in 1883 at the Crown Hotel in Colne Richard Hartley bought Pearson's Farm, two cottages and a further thirty five acres of land. The Hartleys who had retained an interest in Wycoller throughout the centuries were now back as the main landowning family in the valley.

Ghosts and Legends

The boggart tales they used to tell,
  That struck me cold with dread,
On cold, dark nights, with noiseless feet,
  I trembling crept to bed;
To lie awake and frightened hear
  The northern tempest roar.
The ghostly rustle of the blind,
  The sounding great barndoor.
                              A. Wrigley.

Ghost stories and legends cling to the village of Wycoller as they cling to few other villages in the country. Nor is it surprising for this small village, half-hidden and deserted in the twentieth century, has always existed in isolation. Here in a deep sheltered valley surrounded by woods and high moorland was the ideal breeding place for legends. At night in this dark valley it was easy to imagine boggarts on Boulsworth, Guytrash Padfoot waiting in the quiet lanes and the Spectre Horseman galloping down the windswept road.

In *The Annals of Trawden Forest*, Fred Bannister writes, "As the Hall stood massive and lonely and empty for over twenty years before it was dismantled, it would naturally be a fearsome place to the timid who passed on the long dark nights, and the excited fancy would easily people it with the spirits of the departed Cunliffes". However, Wycoller and its ancient hall have been the subject of ghost stories for centuries. On Tuesday, 19 January 1779, Elizabeth Shackleton wrote in her diary, "At ten Cunliffe's servant came with a note to John from Alkincoats, Cunliffe being there to sup, to tell him Mr. T. Clayton and Tom would go to the Haunted House at Wycoller to eat a barrel or two of oysters—desired John and Mr. Shackleton to join them". Elizabeth Shackleton knew the ghost stories of Wycoller Hall well enough to refer to it casually as the Haunted House, it is a pity that she did not say more.

"You may laugh at me: once I should have laughed at the conceit myself, but I've lived so long near Wycoller, suffered there so much and found it the very home of ghosts and hobgoblins.

Believe me, I've heard Guytrash rushing down the winter winds". Author, Halliwell Sutcliffe, put these words into the mouth of one of the characters in his novel *Through Sorrow's Gates*. Halliwell Sutcliffe knew Wycoller well, he wandered in the village and tramped the moorland around it. He listened to the stories of the local people and stored them to use in his novels.

Guytrash—the very word conjures up a revolting image. This north country spirit often referred to simply as "Trash", was also known as Guytrash Padfoot. It appeared in the form of a horse or dog but, as the name Padfoot implies, the dog spirit was the most commonly known. This fiendish hound appeared after dark in lonely lanes and field-paths. The inhabitants of Wycoller feared to meet Guytrash in the lonely lane leading down from Height Laithe to the Hall, up the Dene towards Parson Lee, and in the countless field-paths that led from farm to farm and cottage to cottage.

Guytrash

Charlotte Brontë knew of Guytrash well. Mrs. Gaskell tells us that, "all the grim superstitions of the North had been implanted in her during her childhood by the servants who believed in them". The truth of this is revealed in *Jane Eyre* where Charlotte writes:

> *As this horse approached, and as I watched for it to appear through the dusk, I remembered certain of Bessie's tales, wherein figured a North-of-England spirit, called a 'Gytrash'; which, in the form of horse, mule, or large dog, haunted solitary ways, and sometimes came upon belated travellers, as this horse was now coming upon me.*
>
> *It was very near, but not yet in sight; when, in addition to the tramp, tramp, I heard a rush under the hedge, and close down by the hazel stems glided a great dog, whose black and white colour made him a distinct object against the trees. It was exactly one mask of Bessie's Gytrash—a lion-like creature with long hair and a huge head; it passed me, however, quietly enough; not staying to look up, with strange precanine eyes, in my face as I half expected it would. The horse followed—a tall steed, and on its back a rider. The man, the human being, broke the spell at once. Nothing ever rode the Gytrash; it was always alone.*

In this case the dog was Pilot and the rider Mr. Rochester. A mixture of omens and superstitions, this event gave hints to the further development of the story. Guytrash, the spectre-hound was reputed to have huge saucer-like eyes and its very presence heralded disaster. Mr. Rochester was made to have a nasty fall merely at the symbolic appearance of the spectre-dog. Guytrash was also known locally as "Shriker" or "Skriker" because of its shrieking. Its appearance was also considered to be a warning of the impending death of a relative or friend and any attempt to interfere with it was believed to be fatal.

The Spectre Horseman

Wycoller's most famous ghost is without doubt the Spectre Horseman and it is possible that its origin is related to the Guytrash ghost. Earliest tradition says that he appears on only one evening each year and then only when the weather is at its worst and the wind wild and tempestuous. On such evenings when there was no moon to light the lonely roads the inhabitants of Wycoller hardly dared to venture from their cottages. This tradition was recorded in 1882 by Harland and Wilkinson in *Lancashire Legends*.

> *He is attired in the costume of the early Stuart period and the trappings of his horse are of the most uncouth description. When the wind howls the loudest the horseman can be heard dashing up the road at full speed, and after crossing the narrow bridge, he suddenly stops at the door of the hall. The rider then dismounts and makes his way up the broad open stairs into one of the rooms of the house. Dreadful screams, as from a woman, are then heard, which soon subside into groans. The horseman then makes his appearance at the door—at once mounts his steed—and gallops off the road he came. His body can be seen through by those who may chance to be present; his horse appears to be wild with rage and its nostrils steam with fire.*

The basic story is that one of the Cunliffes murdered his wife in an upstairs bedroom at the Hall, and that the Spectre Horseman is the

The Spectre Horseman—an illustration by Charles Green

ghost of the murderer who is doomed for all eternity to pay an annual visit to the scene of the crime.

We owe a second version of the story to the novelist Halliwell Sutcliffe. In *Mistress Barbara Cunliffe* he placed the event in the reign of Charles II. Stephen Royd tells Barbara Cunliffe the story as they explore the ruins of Wycoller Hall.

> *Well, he went a-hunting once on a day—it was in Charles the Second's time, we're told—and the fox led them a five-mile chase across the moors until he came to Wycoller Dene. He crossed the stream between the straight bridge and the double-arched, and would have turned down the village; but the hounds headed him, and he ran straight as a die through the open main door of the hall, and up the stair here: the hounds followed, and after them the old Squire spurred his horse right up the stair, and into his wife's room, where she had been busy with her tiring maid until the entry of the fox disturbed them. The wife screamed aloud in terror—for the hounds' teeth were already in the fox, and the music of the hunt was deafening—and Simon Cunliffe swore a great oath, and cursed her chicken-heartedness, and raised his hunting-crop as if to strike her. That and the fright together killed her, so they say, and all in haste the Squire drove out the hounds, lest they should turn upon his fallen lady.*

In this story we are told that the ghost is that of Simon Cunliffe, but it must be remembered that Simon Cunliffe is a fictitious character and never existed as a squire at Wycoller Hall.

The last version of the Spectre Horseman story is told in narrative verse by poet, dramatist and composer, Frank Slater. He introduces a new slant to the story. The squire finding his wife alone with a stranger in her bedroom kills her in a fit of jealousy, only to discover that the suspected lover was her brother. It is interesting to note that this was written by Frank Slater on his death-bed in 1918. Too ill to write he dictated his composition—the last thing he felt compelled to do was to complete this narrative poem. The poem is included in the literature section.

A further ghost story is closely connected with the last one. This is the story of the Lady in Black, Black Bess or Old Bess as she is variously known. The lady was first seen in the Hall where she is supposed to have disturbed two lovers. She was dressed from head to foot in black silk—hence her name. The ghostly apparition was completely silent and left after a few moments. She is reputed to be

Black Bess

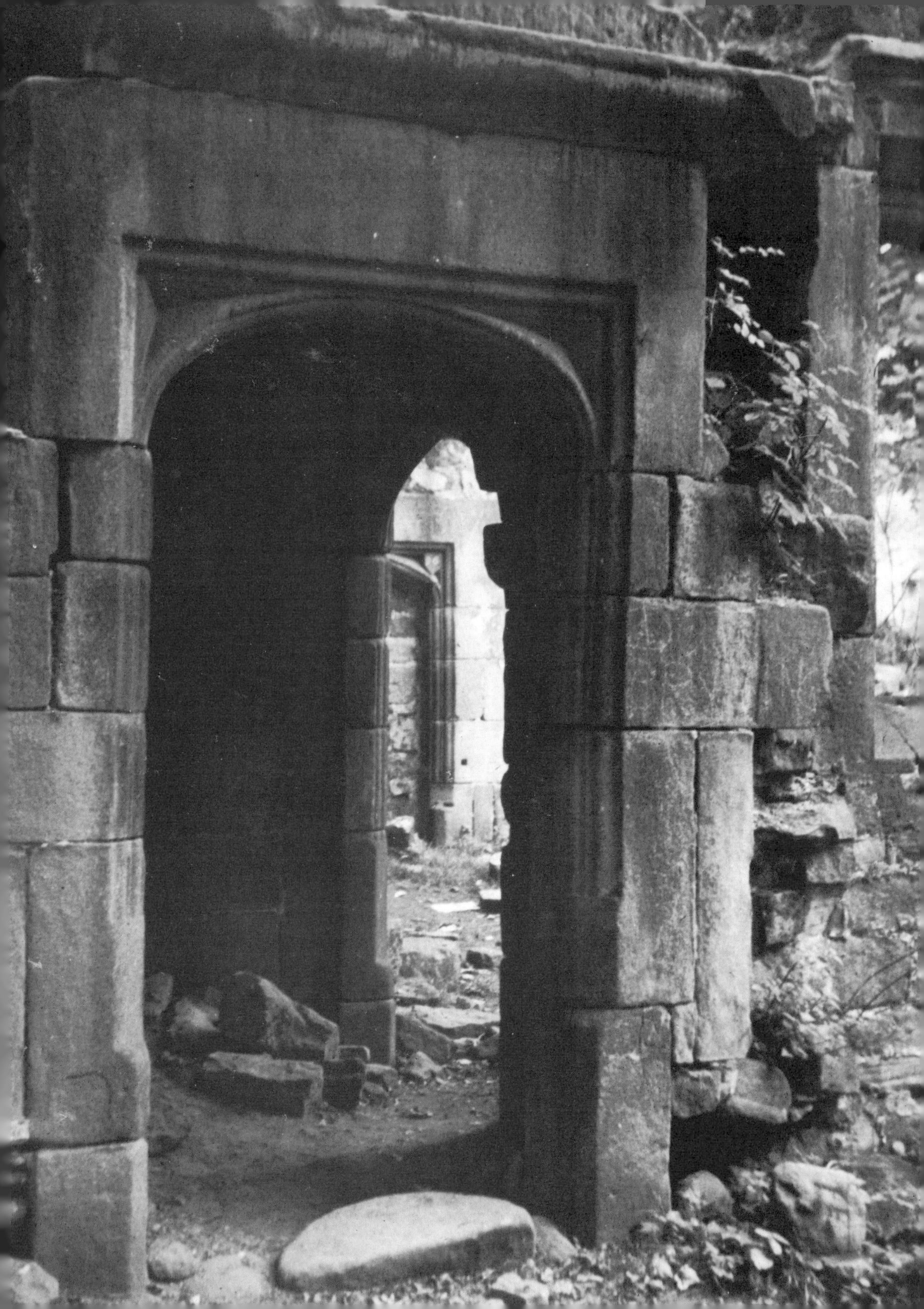

the wife of the Spectre Horseman. Many years ago a second courting couple, sitting on a seat outside the Hall were disturbed by a lady in black. Due to the lady's disappearance the couple did not resume their courting but made a hurried departure from Wycoller. The couple, who lived in Trawden, are both now dead, but they always maintained their story and it is confirmed by their children. It was reported that she was seen by the pack-horse bridge some years ago by two workmen who spoke to her and were then amazed at her sudden disappearance. It was only then that they began to question her strange dress and came to consider that they had truly seen the ghost of Black Bess.

Fred Bannister records a most unusual version of the story in *The Annals of Trawden Forest*. The story begins in the West Indies where one of the Cunliffes is said to have married a West Indian woman. The story goes that on his way back home he began to regret his hasty marriage to a coloured bride and threw her overboard causing her to drown. The spirit of the drowned woman, a true Black Bess, followed him back to Wycoller Hall and there she appears from time to time in search of the man who was responsible for her death.

The ghostly accounts we have considered are relatively distant. They are mainly stories from bygone days, some of them passed down from generation to generation by word of mouth and often embellished by poet and novelist along the way. However, there are other accounts of supernatural activity in Wycoller, accounts substantiated by living people. These ghostly activities were experienced in and around the old farms and cottages during the last forty years.

Frank and Nesta Dewhurst had not lived long at Wycoller House before they became aware of a strange atmosphere in the building. Both of them regularly heard footsteps, most frequently on the staircase in the early morning. At first they were certain that someone must be in the house but, after many searches, soon became accustomed to the unusual noises. Frequently the door to the lounge would open when no one was near to it. It could have been a draught or the door may have been unbalanced but it was neither. As the handle moved and the door opened Frank Dewhurst would sometimes make some comment such as, "It would be nice if you closed the door behind you."

Frank Dewhurst was not a man to be easily affected, not a ready

(Left) A portal to legend—the entrance to Wycoller Hall

The interior of Wycoller House a site of supernatural visitations

believer in ghosts or hauntings yet repeated happenings began to have an effect on his health. People manhandled in an empty room, candles snuffed out, strange noises, all these were the unexplained manifestations of Wycoller House. The Dewhursts' niece Shirley Wilkinson, saw a lady in blue pass in front of her as she came down the stairs. At first she thought it was her mother but then found her mother in a different part of the house. For a time she was convinced that the family were playing a trick on her as the lady in blue disappeared. "It could hardly have been my imagination because I don't believe in ghosts walking about," she explained.

Frank and Nesta Dewhurst saw nothing in the house, but their small daughter, Judith, who was only three when they took up residence at Wycoller, did. They were convinced that she was the constant target of whatever it was that shared their tenancy. From the first innocuous seeming appearances these gradually developed to far more frightening things, so that she was becoming increasingly nervous. At one time the girl asked her mother who came to see her every night, but when her mother explained that it was she the girl wanted to know who came afterwards. Not wanting to frighten the child the mother told her that it was probably her guardian angel, but the guardian angel often took on frightening forms. The girl described one apparition in her childish language as "A man wearing two hats—one round and a square one on top—and a long black cloak, with no hands and feet, and no eyes only windows". A friend of the family contacted a psychic research organisation who sent a representative to visit the house. From this time the family no longer regarded the haunting in any humorous light and shortly afterwards left the village. No member of the family has had any similar experiences at any other place than Wycoller.

Lowlands Farm, the home of Alfred Wilkinson, has also been subject to unexplainable happenings. Alfred Wilkinson reported that occasionally while doing the evening milking in the shippon the door had unexplicably opened and closed. He had spoken and looked up but there was never anyone there. Similar experiences had been reported by his father when he lived in Wycoller many years before.

Pearson's Farm has also been claimed to be the site of supernatural activities. The manifestations reported by two witnesses and described in similar terms are reported to take place in the older part of the building. However, they were experienced by people living in the more modern house next door. The first witness was an old lady who was lying ill in the downstairs room and told visitors that the house was haunted. She said that whatever they were they came through into the room where she was sleeping. Many years later a girl sleeping in an upstairs room in the same house gave a very similar description of noises and disturbances that she heard in the night.

Farmer William Bracewell, was troubled with noises and bumps in the night when he lived in the same building then called Wycoller Farm. Probably the most scaring incident was experienced by his son, Kenneth. He stayed up late one night with a farrowing sow in the barn next to the old Hall and while there he distinctly heard footsteps approaching. He spoke thinking that it was his father, and then turned to find no one there. He ran back to the house to find

Hauntings have been reported at Pearson's Farm

that his father was fast asleep. William Bracewell never worried about hauntings for as he told reporters he was "middlin hard".

One of the last occupiers of the house talks of seeing the shadow of a tall broad-shouldered man against the wall to the right of the fire-place in the sitting room when she was alone one evening. She was terrified thinking that some stranger had got into the house but turning she saw that there was no one there—nothing but a shape, hanging flimsily and darkly transparent, before her. The shadow was shaped like a man yet without anything solid to provide its source. She regarded it steadily for an unmarked period of time, and presently it faded, appearing to dissolve into the wall.

We leave the ghosts now to take a look at some of the legends of Wycoller and the surrounding area. In a newspaper article many years ago Fred Bannister wrote about the lad of Crow Hill. A lad wandering on the moors in very bad weather had lost his way. Overcome with exhaustion he sat down on Crow Hill and there died of exposure. When his skeleton was discovered there was an argument between the parishes of Haworth, Stanbury and Trawden as to who should bury him. The Trawden authorities said the place was beyond their boundary, but eventually they agreed to accept the trouble and expense of burying the skeleton. Having buried the remains and raised a stone they then claimed that the boundary should be altered to bring the grave within Trawden. Fred Bannister says, "The gravestone is still there, on the flat of the moor, and bearing the inscription, Lad or Scar on Crow Hill". An unknown poet wrote the following verse about the gravestone:

The Lad of Crow Hill

> Sing me dirges, grouse and plover,
>   When the moor is painted over
> With the purple of the heather,
>   Snow in windy, wintry weather
> Lightly press on my body here,
>   This is its bed from year to year.

The Lad of Crow Hill

Perhaps the poet's muse would not have responded had he known that the gravestone was simply a boundary mark placed there to mark the boundary between Wycoller and Oakworth pastures. This legend like many others melts away in the face of hard facts. The facts are these: in 1788 Henry Own Cunliffe was in court at York defending himself against a claim of land on the Wycoller boundary. The brief for the defendant makes a strong opening claim that, "The natural appearance of the place in dispute, if there were no evidence to confirm it, is very strong in favour of the Wycoller Line". It explains how the boundary leads from one stone to another along to Crow Hill. "The Lad or Scarth or Scarche upon Crowhill was a Quantity of loose stones piled up upon a heap, so as to make a small piked hill, after the manner of the Lawes upon the Borders of Scotland, and was standing until four or five years ago. It was privately removed, but by whom it is not known, tho, its being claimed by Wycoller as a Mear affords pretty strong tho silent Evidence".

So the plaintiffs were accused of removing the Lad of Crow Hill. The defendants case was summed up as follows, "Unless the Hanging Stone or Watershackles Cross, Standing Stone, and Lad or Scarche on Crowhill, but particularly the two former were placed as Boundary marks, it is totally impossible to account for their appearing in the situation in which they are found to be". Henry Owen Cunliffe won his case and the Lad of Crow Hill was replaced with an engraved stone, the likeness of which to a rounded gravestone gave rise to the legend.

Lad Law

A similar misleading explanation occurs in *Memories of Hurstwood* by T. T. Wilkinson. He says, "in the direction of Boulsworth is a large block of millstone grit named 'Llad Law'. The prefix 'Llad' is a pure Celtic word, signifying to 'kill' or slaughter, while the affix 'Law' is the Saxon 'Lleow', or hill, 'the Hill of Slaughter'; pointing in an unmistakable manner, to the time when the Druids offered human sacrifices on their sacred rock". The stone once again is a boundary mark and Lad and Law are both words signifying nothing more than this, as seen from the legal document of 1788. The story is the result of misunderstood word origins coupled with an over romantic imagination.

There is also a legend that a skeleton was once found in a sitting position against a large stone immediately in front of Lad Law. The skeleton was said to be that of a man who had lost his way, wandered

Weathered shapes of outcrop rock on Boulsworth Hill

Lad Law

over the moor until he was exhausted and then sat down there to die. The stone was said to be clearly stained with an impression of the body that could not be removed. There is no trace today!

The introduction of altars and Druids takes us back to *Romantic Wycoller* where E. W. Folley writes, "the highest eminence, being nearest to the sky, to the heavens, became sacred as a place of worship. So the hill communities gathering together for safety found themselves in a temple and erected stones or altars to mark the spot. Worship and work went hand in hand". Once again *Romantic Wycoller* is being romantic in name and romantic in nature. Many of the stones referred to by E. W. Folley are boundary markers while others are purely the accidental weathered shapes of outcrop rock. How easy to imagine these as altars and to see the natural potholes in their surface as bowls cut by the Druids to hold the blood of sacrificed victims or to collect pure water for use in their religious ceremonies. Peter Wightman in *Whalley to Wycoller* stretched romance and imagination to the extreme when he wrote:

> *The Druids, that mysterious body of priests who were skilled in astrology, sorcery and witchcraft, are reputed to have been established in this village and to have used the many bridges to reach the amphitheatre where human sacrifices took place. A bridge of huge stones called the "Druids' Bridge" still crosses the stream at Wycoller.*

Foster's Leap

A further legend concerns the rocks at Foster Leap on the hillside near Foster Leap Farm. According to the story the name, now applied to a farm and several fields, was given to the rocks after Foster Cunliffe, a relative of the Cunliffes of Wycoller Hall, leapt across either for a bet or as an act of bravado. The first appearance of the name Foster Leap found in the research for this book occurs in the Baptism Registers of Colne Parish Church in 1714. Research also shows that Foster Cunliffe, the only son of Ellis Cunliffe was born in 1685 and died in 1758. Foster's father was a Chaplain to King Charles II and it is reputed that the king himself was Foster's god-father. There is no evidence to show that Foster Cunliffe ever visited Wycoller but it is quite possible. He became a wealthy merchant in Liverpool and from the account of Thomas Eyre we know that he was instrumental in finding a position for young Henry Cunliffe, who later became the Squire at Wycoller Hall.

So here is a legend that may well be founded on fact. The second story relating to Foster Leap is less likely to be so. The story tells of a sheep stealer who having been caught in Wycoller was offered an alternative to the normal routine justice. If he could jump the rocks at Foster Leap he would be freed. It is said that the thief, on horseback, leapt the gap from rock to rock but, being unable to halt on the other side, both horse and rider fell to their deaths.

The story of Foster Cunliffe and Foster Leap brought Charles II into the picture. The following story brings Charles II to Wycoller Hall. The story which appeared in *The Colne and Nelson Times* in 1930 was signed William Makin, Wycoller Old Hall, Trawden, Near Colne. The writer explains that Wycoller Hall was formerly called Abbeydean.

A most unlikely story

It appears that these people laboured many years to build themselves a home, and the fruit of their labours was the beautiful building, which they christened Abbeydean Manor, They were enjoying the results of their labours and living all very happily, until one day King Charles arrived at the Manor, just after his return as King. He and his Royal entourage stayed two days and two nights at the Manor. It appears that after having feasted and drank he decreed that a hunting party should be made up at once, and this, of course, was heartily approved of by all, with the exception of one of the Royal party, a German duke, and one of the young hot-bloods of the house family. These two complained of being too tired to join the hunt party, so they stayed at home and sat in the fireplace and played games. The chit-chat was upon the subject of dress and horses, and finally turned to religion. The German duke was a sworn Catholic, and the young son of the home family following his parents' religion, that of a true Protestant Church of England. Some unknown remark was made between them, with the result that the German duke spat a mouthful of tobacco juice into the face of the other.

The story continues that a fight took place between the young Cunliffe and the duke. Later when the King returned with the hunting party he was enraged to hear of the trouble and swore that the family and servants should become Catholics within the next twenty four hours. For refusing they had all their possessions destroyed before the King's party left.

The King granted them no mercy whatever, and they were turned out of their home ... Everything was destroyed and then burned ... The name of Wycoller Hall originated upon the incident of the family being turned out of the Manor. Before leaving they sought an interview with the King, and said to him, in their pleadings for mercy and shelter, "We have never done you any harm, and we are your most loyal subjects, and simply because we cannot bring ourselves to forsake our Father in heaven, 'why collar all' we have on earth?" These simple spoken words were the real original re-naming of the Manor from Abbeydean Manor to Why-Collar-All.

The editor of the newspaper wisely stated that he published the letter as a matter of interest but declined any editorial responsibility for the theory put forward by the writer. This is surely the most fanciful story of Wycollar ever to be fabricated.

As you have seen some legends can be investigated and their origins revealed but ghost stories are a different matter. You must come to your own conclusions about the Wycoller ghosts. Perhaps when the village is brought back to life the old ghosts will re-appear.

Wycoller in Literature

How I have loved the mossy earth beneath my feet,
And loved the glossy meadowlands with lush grass sweet
Whilst I have lingered long beside those ferny streams
That murmur through the valley, home of happy dreams;
And I have never wished to journey far from here,
No other place has ever seemed one half so dear.
                    The Charm of Wycoller, Nesta Wood.

Wycoller's charm has influenced, poets, playwrights and novelists alike. What is this charm, the charisma of this secluded moorland valley? Perhaps it is the contrast of the attractive fertile valley with the wild rough moorland that surrounds it. Perhaps it is the contrast of this calm and peaceful dene with the noise and bustle of the factory towns that lie not far away. Wycoller also symbolises the rural village from which all our ancestors came—a rural haven sucked dry by the Industrial Revolution's insatiable appetite for factory workers. The fact that for over a century, year by year the village has slowly fallen into ruin is a further aspect of its charm. Here was the romantic appeal of desolation, the deserted village, the lost people, the haunt of ghosts. Here visitors have sensed a return to the past and enjoyed the peace of rural England.

Nesta Wood   Nesta Wood lived in Wycoller for many years and translated the beauty and spirit of the valley into poetry. A published collection of her poems, *Visions and Voices* contains several poems about Wycoller. In the preface of the book, E. W. Folley wrote: "Endowed with a gift of imagination and love of words, Nesta Wood has produced here a work of extraordinary merit, aided by the magic of her word music we see the invisible . . . Not only poetry lovers but many others should derive from this book sustained enjoyment".

(Right) Nesta Wood in the porch of Wycoller House

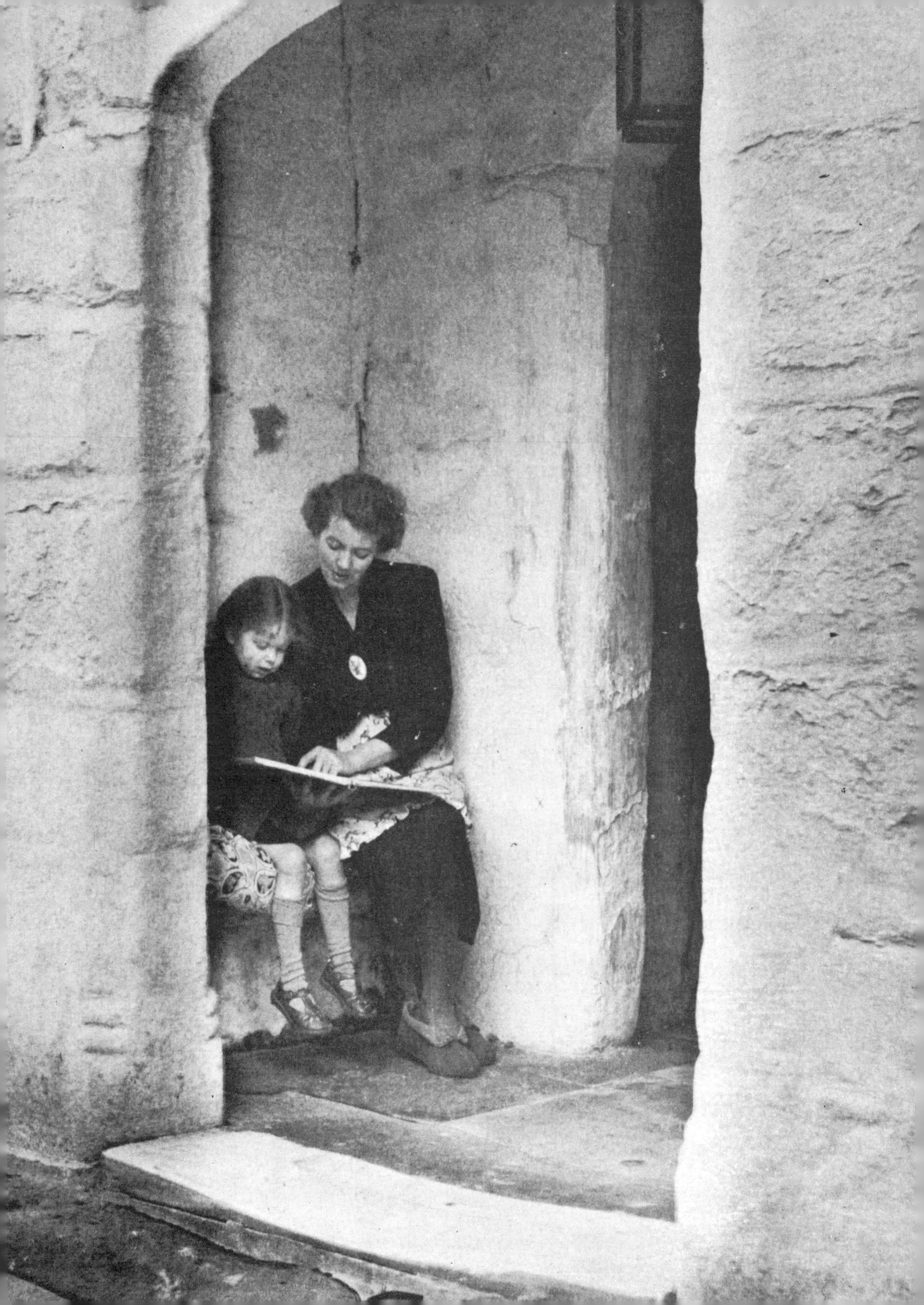

THE CHARM OF WYCOLLER

*I have come singing when red sun of evening skies
Has made enchantment manifest before my eyes;
When fresh from day-long roving over wind-swept heights,
Half drunk with air and distances and pure delights,
With silent laughter having trod by moorland streams,
I stand within the valley of my youthful dreams,*

*With gladness they have greeted me, the spirits there,
The joyous sounds of welcoming have filled the air;
And I have thrown my arms in love about a tree—
So well beloved are all, so beautiful to me—
And listened with my cheek against the deep-scarred bark
To the celestial singing of an angel lark.*

*How I have loved the mossy earth beneath my feet,
And loved the glossy meadowlands with lush grass sweet
Whilst I have lingered long beside those ferny streams
That murmur through the valley, home of happy dreams;
And I have never wished to journey far from here,
No other place has ever seemed one half so dear.*

*So I come singing to that ever sacred place
Whose peace has clothed my spirit with its timeless grace.*

REFLECTIONS ON WYCOLLER HALL

How like a dream, this home of long ago
In emptiness to end, as most dreams do!
These walls are silent yet so much they know
Of those who loved and vanished, false and true,
Who in loud laughter or 'mid sorrow's tears
Raised echoes to the roof which is no more,
Or strong in youth, feet light upon this floor
Thought little of the passing of the years.

But Time makes all things bow; no joys remain;
All leave their loves, however strong, to fade,
Nor man nor maid has lived to prove this vain
For Time's hand gathers all, and go we must.
So was it here — the gallant show they made
Is lost for ever in the ageing dust.

Though seasons change the changeless scene,
Her wintry charms are no less sweet,
With snow composed of countless gems
She lays a carpet for our feet,
And mantles every smallest twig
In raiment delicate and neat.

And softly, sadly drapes the stone
Of long-abandoned Hall,
Whose many years and yesterdays
Are gone beyond recall.
                              Reminiscence

A WYCOLLER ADVENTURE

Through Wycoller rambled three jovial men
Old Sammy, John Thomas and Timothy Lee,
That night they had toasted their fellow-men
And lifted their tankards again and again
So full of convivial pleasure just then
Were old Sammy, John Thomas and Timothy Lee.

On the old pack-horse bridge they sat down to rest,
Old Sammy, John Thomas and Timothy Lee
And each began to unburden his breast,
For each was a hero by others unguessed.
How strange that the world remained unimpressed
By old Sammy, John Thomas and Timothy Lee!

The hours slipped by as their stories they told,
Old Sammy, John Thomas and Timothy Lee
For one was a soldier so fearless and bold,
Another a statesman both peerless and cold,
And here was one with great plans to unfold,
Old Sammy, John Thomas and Timothy Lee.

And glibly they talked in the moon's pallid gleam,
Old Sammy, John Thomas and Timothy Lee
Quite lost in a grand and beautiful dream
Until altogether they gave a great scream,
Leapt up in a panic and fell into the stream,
Old Sammy, John Thomas and Timothy Lee.

The reason was this: they had seen a strange sight
Old Sammy, John Thomas and Timothy Lee,
A great ghostly horseman came out of the night
And galloped towards them in shadow and light,
Their hair stood on end in frenzy and fright,
Old Sammy, John Thomas and Timothy Lee.

They crouched in the stream by common consent,
Old Sammy, John Thomas and Timothy Lee,
As over the bridge the gaunt horseman went
And never a sound those flying hoofs sent,
No stopping to argue and maybe repent
For old Sammy, John Thomas and Timothy Lee.

At length from the water they scrambled those three,
Old Sammy, John Thomas and Timothy Lee,
And wordless, were off as fast as could be,
With a trembling of limb and a weakness of knee:

But only the moon was present to see
Old Sammy, John Thomas and Timothy Lee.

HARD WINTER

Hard sky — iron hard — and snow
Piled wall-top high;
Icycles in gleaming ranks
Along the frozen river's banks—
And Spring not nigh

Trees, etched whitely, motionless
In death-like sleep;
Birds, dull-plumaged, glazed of eye,
Just dropping, freezing where they lie,
For death to keep.

Rabbits crouching at my door
In limp despair,
Craving sustenance and ease:
Stark evidence of bark-stripped trees,
No comfort there.

Week, after week, after week—
And then, the sun,
Lavish in redeemer's role,
Will take no count of Winter's toll,
For what is done, is done!

Born in Staffordshire, Frank Slater came to Burnley in Lancashire with his parents at the age of two years. Early in his adult life he moved to Colne and it was there he settled and fulfilled his musical ambitions. He was a keen song writer, composer and choirmaster. He is most remembered for his *Bonnie Colne* written in 1873 but he composed *Victoria Jubilate* for Queen Victoria's Diamond Jubilee and *Colunio* to commemorate Colne's incorporation as a Borough.

He wrote several plays including *Grassington, Monkroyd, Walverden* and *Wycoller Dene*. These plays are an escape to rural simplicity

Frank Slater

> **Theatre Royal, Colne.** MONDAY, DEC. 6, 1897,
> And during the week.
>
> After the lapse of nine years,
> ### THE COLNE VOCAL HARMONISTS
> Have the pleasure to announce that they will re-produce
> Mr. Frank Slater's ever-welcome Local Drama in 4 Acts, entitled:—
> ## "WYCOLLAR DENE."
> BRIGHT COSTUMES.   TUNEFUL MUSIC.   SPLENDID CASTE.
>
> Squire Cunliffe: "Now then Buckthorn, lad, this is welcome news is it not?"
> Buckthorn: "Yes it is, Squire, and likely news for sport, depend on it!"—
> *Act 1, Scene 3.*
>
> Centre Circle, 1/6; Balconies and Stalls, 1/-; Pit, 6d. Open, 6-45; Curtain rise, 7-30; Saturday 6-15, Curtain rise 7-0.
>
> See Posters.   Business Secretary, MR. HARRY NUTTER.

where peasant folk overcome temporary wickedness and settle back to an idyllic life. The plays were enjoyed in Victorian Colne and from time to time they have been produced since. *Wycoller Dene* was produced by Colne Operatic Society to assist the funds of the Friends of Wycoller.

Wycoller Dene was written in the eighteen nineties and was produced in Colne's Victorian theatres. It was always popular because of its local appeal, its bright costumes and its attractive music. The events of the story take place in the rural seclusion of Wycoller Dene some centuries ago. The opening scene is on the village green where shepherds and peasants have gathered to celebrate a sheep-shearing festival.

Bertha Dene, the niece of Squire Cunliffe of Wycoller Hall, had two rival suitors, Cecil Stanley an aristocrat and Squire Hollinhall an adventurer from Trawden Forest. Squire Hollinhall schemes to marry Bertha and so gain Wycoller Hall and the Cunliffe estate. Paul Ravenrock once Hollinhall's accomplice refuses to help him and in fact decided to frustrate his plans. Squire Cunliffe challenges Hollinhall to a cock-fight for a heavy wager. Hollinhall accepts and gets two country yokels, Brackenhill and Thorneyhedge, to drug Squire Cunliffe's birds. Cunliffe loses the battle and to save him from debt Bertha Dene promises to marry Squire Hollinhall.

However, Paul Ravenrock and Jim Buckthorn appear on the scene and reveal his treachery. Ravenrock and Hollinhall fight a duel and the wicked Hollinhall is slain. All ends well, Squire Cunliffe regains Wycoller Hall, and his niece, Bertha, is able to marry the man of her choice.

The subsidiary plot is a sheep-stealing intrigue. Two shepherds, Harry Fosterleap and Tom Smithyclough, are rivals for the love of a local shepherdess, Bess Lingfeather. Bess's favourite, Harry Fosterleap, is sent to Lancaster on a charge of sheep stealing. Tom Smithyclough is responsible for the charge and Harry is sent to prison. However, he is proved innocent, Tom Smithyclough is drowned in a flood at Crow Hill and Bess Lingfeather is reunited with her lover in fair Wycoller Dene. The scenes are set at Wycoller Hall, the Herders Inn, the old prison in Colne and other places in and around Wycoller. The dramatist draws the names of his characters from the local farms and countryside and what colourful and fascinating names they are, Ravenrock, Fosterleap, Smithyclough and Brackenhills.

Frank Slater's *Spectre Horseman* was published in 1918, the year of his death and the original version is included here with the exception of a few repetitive verses.

Frank Slater at Foster's Leap

THE SPECTRE HORSEMAN
by Frank Slater

No fairer sight was ever seen
On any English village green,
Than when the lads and lasses gay
Once sped to greet their Queen of May.
    In fair Wycoller Dene.

The Squire had won the lovliest bride
That ever touched man's heart with pride;
And he, to celebrate the day,
Would have crowned her the Queen of May,
    Upon the village green.

The hillside rang with merry joy,
As milkmaid, hind and shepherd boy
Resolved to spend the happiest day
    Of all bright summer's round.

And when arrived upon the green,
Ah! who could paint so fair a scene?
Not rosiest garland woven there
Could with her rosy cheeks compare,
    Upon that happy sylvan ground.

And there, enthroned within a bower,
Sat she, the Queen of that brief hour;
So sweet the grace she did impart,
Her smile went straight to every heart
    That there its homage paid.

The Squire was filled with deep delight
As, gazing on a scene so bright,
He saw their guileless hearts were given
To her, who was his earthly heaven,
    And there his happy heart was laid.

*The feast grew merrier hour by hour,
As round about the regal bower
The merry maidens of the Dene
Sang out the praises of their Queen,
    Their bonny smiling Queen of May.*

*But never day saw morning light
That did not yield to coming night;
And that glad day came to an end,
As homewards did the peasants wend,
    Before they were benighted.*

*Yet ah! the serpent as of old,
Had crept into that peaceful fold:
A secret meeting had been seen
In depth of orchard's bowery green.*

*The Squire, in passing near one night,
Saw approach a vision bright;
It was his love, his joy, his pride;
But why alone at eventide?*

*He turned his head to see her go,
And there, amazed, beyond he saw
A youth awaiting her to come—
Of secret motives they had none.*

*He saw them meet in fond embrace,
By this to him she lost all grace;
He saw her give him well-filled purse,
For this she earned his bitter curse.*

*Had then the Squire resolved to go
And learn the truth of all he saw,
He would have found no secret lover
But, to his joy, her own dear brother.*

*With feet deformed from very birth,
He could not walk old mother earth;
She helped him mount and saw him start
Towards his native Haworth home.*

*His sister turned like ariel sprite,
Went tripping through the misty night
To that dear home she loved so well,
And where she hoped for long to dwell.*

*By flood of jealous rage possessed,
All reason gone, with heaving breast,
On stalked the Squire towards the hall,
Resolved that night to end it all.*

*He rushed into her cosy room,
And in his face she saw her doom;
She shrieked and ran towards the door,
But there with butt of dog-whip raised
He struck her dead unto the floor.*

*He gazed upon his heinous crime,
The tale of which will last all time;
Remorse then gripped him heart and soul,
Why had he done a deed so foul?*

*What proof had he of wrong she'd done?
Returning reason answered—none.
He bounded down the old oak stair,
And reached his hunter's stable door,
He mounted there his swiftest steed,
Then fled, and never was seen more.*

*The legend says that once a year
He must return and re-appear,
Fleshless rider, fleshless steed,
Come down the lane at headlong speed,
To re-enact his awful deed.*

*Re-entering once again the hall,
A shriek is heard and then a fall;
Re-mounting, up the Dene he goes,
Where to, no mortal being knows:
His long atonement now at end
He seeks no face of foe or friend.*

Those days have long since passed away,
The Dene now knows a brighter day,
Where children's laughter can be heard
Mingling with the song of bird.

A labyrinth of o'erspreading trees
Gives grateful shade from sun or breeze,
A lovlier spot there could not be
To those who wish to go and see.

Embosomed in the valley deep,
Long may thy secret beauty keep;
To all appreciative eyes
Disclose thy beauty and surprise.

A place of rest for weary brain,
Who see thee once will see again;
Remain as thou hast ever been,
Lovely, fair Wycoller Dene.

* * * *

On Hallow's Eve, when brown October dies,
And drear November bids her storms arise,
When stormy blasts without do roar,
With shutters fast and locked the door,
In memory of the virtuous dead
Let this legend then be read.

Two books exist published by Emmotts Wycoller: *Eamot Eternal* in 1952 and *An Outlaw in the Twentieth Century* in 1964. Both these books were written and published by Thomas Clifford Emmott; the first an unusual novel and the second an even more unusual autobiography. The books were published from Wycoller Cottage where Tom Emmott lived for so long that the cottage became known as Emmott's Cottage.

In his autobiography Tom Emmott tells us that his family came to Burnley when he was a boy and that he was educated at Arnold House School in Blackpool and Ashville Methodist College at Harrogate. Tom Emmott gives a dramatic description of how he first

Tom Emmott

Tom Emmott outside his Wycoller Cottage

came to Wycoller during the severe winter of 1947: "I was on a ramble to Haworth, we faced a blizzard on our way back. Sven, a late Norwegian Commando in the resistance movement, Tan, a Chinese gentleman, who had fought in the mountains of China against the Japanese . . . were in the party. They dropped behind me in a file; I was accepted as their leader . . . It was terrible, Arctic, on those heights". He tells us that the landlord's wife at the Herders Inn told him of a vacant cottage in the valley and that he came to view it.

Whatever the truth of the discovery, Tom Emmott found his dream cottage in Wycoller and overcame many obstacles to become its tenant. The walls were bare of plaster, grass grew between the flags that covered the floor and the kitchen fire-place was a mass of crumbled stone and rusted iron work. He tells us: "I fell in love with the house, and have now lived here seventeen years of grief, happiness and drama, but always there has been the peace which passeth all understanding".

Emmott was very keen on camping and all out of door activities and tells us that he was present at the First World Conference of Camping where Prince Leopold of Belgium sat in his tent and awarded him first prize and a medal for the best camp outfit. During the same period he says that he camped with the Northern Cave and Fell Club and mapped all the underground caves in the Ingleborough and Whernside area. Later he proposed an organisation to provide overnight lodgings for ramblers, and he tells us that the result was the founding of the Youth Hostels Association. He recounts among other things that he trained as a parachutist, that he smuggled secret film out of Germany in his tent pole, that he was in Military Intelligence, that he attended Sandhurst Military College and became a commissioned officer, that he passed countless examinations in art, commercial law and business activities, that he had a degree in psychology from London University, and that his economic plans had been forwarded to the World Monetary Conference by the Chancellor of the Exchequer.

Many people were impressed by this record and thought what a remarkable fellow Tom Emmott was. In 1964, following his death, it was proposed within Colne Council that Wycoller should be preserved as a monument to him. But Tom Emmott did too well and when some of his claims were checked it was discovered that Tom Emmott did not have a degree in psychology and that he had not

Granada Marathon during the 1959 General Election

Lancastrian Party

served in Military Intelligence. Tom Emmott appears to have been self-centred, vain and suffering from delusions. We have seen a possible expression of his delusions of grandeur in the claims made in his autobiography.

In 1959 he formed the Lancastrian Party in the hope of focussing attention on the neglect of North East Lancashire. He had few active supporters and found it difficult to organise a meeting with more than three or four in attendance. He stood as a prospective M.P., for the Parliamentary Division of Nelson and Colne during the election of 1959 and polled a total of 1,889 votes. Following the 1959 election Tom Emmott's feelings of persecution grew and grew. He claimed that political persecution had stopped people attending his meetings. From this time he felt oppressed by everyone and found it extremely difficult to gain employment. He wrote letters and appeals to local people, the vicar, and to the House of Lords and and the Archbishop of Canterbury. From 1961 he claimed that his physical health had become affected by persecution. When he was refused employment by the personnel officer of a Brierfield company who also recommended that he should see a psychiatrist, Tom Emmott wrote: "I was white with rage, I had been let down. I was speechless with shock and have not been able to speak since".

He remained speechless for some time believing that his persecutors had caused him to be struck dumb. His physical anguish increased from this time and he suffered several accidents.

> *I had been to Colne shopping. The blizzard was starting, I was held up by drifts and before I had traversed the first field darkness fell. The blizzard blanketed all sight; the drifts like a deep blanket blocked my path. I moved forward by instinct as I could see no landmark, my ruc-sac was heavy with groceries. The floor of ice suddenly caved in and I fell through into the river. I lay held down by my ruc-sac straps. I fought desperately, my left arm was pinned under me and had taken the weight of my fall. The cold was uncanny—it felt like an electric shock—I lay in the ice cold water. In total blackness I struggled and in time, an eternity, I released the straps and struggled, prised, fought, and I realised I was in bad trouble. At last I got to my knees. Using each knee in turn I made steps and climbed slowly and with great effort up the black wall of invisible ice and snow. Each step took tremendous effort. It was frightening. I arose slowly from the cruel river; so mild in summer when crowds of happy children play in its water, but now an elemental menace. For a long time I lay in comparative safety, and then pulled myself out of the lethargy of exhaustion which leads to death, felt Dene Cottage gate, and on that aligned my forward route.*

Tom Emmott began planning to form a company to be called, The Drainage Pipe Co., Ltd., of Trawden Forest. He wished to form a public company but several local solicitors refused to register the company. He put it down to the fact that they had been contacted by his political enemies. Not put off, Tom Emmott, retained solicitors Wilkinson and Nolan to work on his behalf and set about interviewing directors for the company. When he received registration documents for a small private company he was disturbed and angry.

> *I am never normally perturbed but this criminal act stunned me. I went outside to put a displaced stone on our wall, went dizzy, fell back, striking my head on the road and damaging my spine. The milk lorry man helped me after I had been there over half-an-hour.*

From then on I had acute pain down my spine, a permanent stiff neck and the ground kept wobbling under me. It was murder by indirect cruelty. No one realised how bad I was. I interviewed our final man who told me he had accepted on the fifteenth. I could not understand why my solicitor had not informed me, this was not reasonable.

Was it that the powers of evil still haunt these Northern Hills? Do witches and things that creep in the night still exist? Warlocks and spooks, goblins and hobgoblins do they still laugh at our self complacent pseudo-Christian charade of cars and electronics. Well, last night I might have believed they were revenging themselves upon me. It happened on the first day we had decided that British political persecution had prevented the formation of the company. I had drafted a letter offering a Consultancy Service and stuck it up outside. Somehow this seemed not in keeping with the lonely night, so I wrote one "Wizard of Wycoller" offering the same service but in a different way. I stuck it on a nail, came in, started to shave, dropped my blade, stooped to pick it up, and slipped on my saliva which is persisting since I hurt my jaw. With my withered arm and my weakness I could not get up. I edged over to the chair inch by inch on the flat of my back, my damaged neck giving out stabs of acute pain. I tried desperately to raise myself by the chair but kept falling back. It was 1.40 p.m.—my wife had gone to work. I edged inch by inch across to the Aga, tried to reach the rail, slipped back. Tried to reach the rail, fell back. Kept on trying, now sweating with strain. Edged half inch by inch on my back to the chair, grabbed a red cushion to put under my throbbing neck (Wilkinson Accident). Realised I needed my stick to knock up door latch. Edged back, taking half-an-hour to do it, to the sink, grabbed my stick. After repeated effort knocked up the latch and the door swung open. An hour later I reached the front door; two men were looking at my book. I could not call out, having no vocal ability, but made bangs on the door and squeaked, "help! help". They laughed and went away. The wind blew the door to, the latch clicked down.

He wrote further on his sufferings listing them together at the end of one chapter.

In my lifetime my body has had some experiences not dwelt on in this story of my life but now recounted; I broke the 2nd vertebra in my spine in road accident while at the Mill, I broke chest ribs and bruised spine and tore heart muscle in the war. Had total acute

EAMOT ETERNAL

By T. C. EMMOTT

TENEZ LE VRAGE!

rheumatism through exposure. Two years not sleeping through shell blast. Four bits of shrapnel in right leg. Total muscular rheumatism caught at Blackpool. St Vitus Dance, three months, cured by mental control. Paralysed tongue and throat muscles as a result of victimisation. Loss of use of arm and hands, and kinetic result of falling in river, etc. during blizzard. That's all but for severe injury to neck, head, spine on Horace Wilkinson's default and wrong action. As a child most childish ailments. My mind has not been touched in any way by my experiences and for this I thank thee my God. I put all this together because I was never one to bother about my pain.

Tom Emmott's novel *Eamot Eternal* follows an expected pattern and traces the Emmott family back to the lost city of Atlantis. Chapter by chapter we see the Emmott family passing through every age—ancient Egypt, Roman times, the Norman period, the Civil War, and on to modern times. In each chapter the hero is Thom Emmott who overcame all. This novel simply says Thomas Emmott is a leader of men, he has always existed and will always exist—Emmott is eternal.

There is no doubt that Tom Emmott had ability, more than average ability. To put two books together and see them through publication takes both ability and persistence. Tom Emmott's autobiography is an attractively produced book with fascinating chapter titles. His type of apparent delusions are frequently found in those of above average ability: the memory remains good, there is no real confusion, lucidity of speech is common but there is no insight. To Thomas Clifford Emmott it was the rest of the world that was out of step. Perhaps Wycoller was one of the few places able to offer him some peace of mind.

Brontë connections

A long tradition connects the Brontë family with Wycoller and each year thousands of Brontë lovers include a visit to Wycoller in search of the Bronte spirit. They come to Wycoller because they have read or heard that the Brontës walked here and knew the village well. They come to revere the ruins of Wycoller Hall as the Ferndean Manor of *Jane Eyre,* believing profoundly that it was from this secluded spot that Charlotte Brontë received a source of inspiration.

> *The manor-house of Ferndean was a building of considerable antiquity, moderate size, and no architectural pretensions, deep buried in a wood. I had heard of it before. Mr. Rochester often spoke of it, and sometimes went there. His father had purchased the estate*

Charlotte Brontë, a portrait by Richmond, National Gallery

for the sake of the game coverts. He would have let the house, but could find no tenant, in consequence of its ineligible and insalubrious site. Ferndean then remained uninhabited and unfurnished with the exception of some two or three rooms fitted up for the accommodation of the squire when he went there in the season to shoot.

To this house I came just ere dark, on an evening marked by the characteristics of sad sky, cold gale, and continued, small penetrating rain. The last mile I performed on foot. having dismissed the chaise and driver with the double remuneration I had promised. Even when within a very short distance of the manor-house, you could see nothing of it, so thick and dark grew the timber of the gloomy wood about it. Iron gates between granite pillars showed me where to enter, and passing through them, I found myself at once in the twilight of close ranked trees. There was a grass-grown track descending the forest aisle, between hoar and knotty shafts and under branched arches. I followed it, expecting soon to reach the dwelling, but it stretched on and on, it wound far and farther: no sign of habitation or grounds was visible.

I thought I had taken a wrong direction and lost my way. The darkness of natural as well as of sylvan dusk gathered over me. I looked round in search of another road. There was none: all was interwoven stem, columnar trunk, dense summer foliage—no opening anywhere.

I proceeded: at last my way opened, the trees thinned a little; presently I beheld a railing, then the house—scarce, by this dim light distinguishable from the trees; so dank and green were its decaying walls. Entering a portal, fastened only by a latch, I stood amidst a space of enclosed ground, from which the wood swept away in a semicircle. There were no flowers, no garden-beds; only a broad gravel walk girdling a grass plot, and this set in the heavy frame of the forest. The house presented two pointed gables in its front; the windows were latticed and narrow, the front-door was narrow too, one step led up to it. The whole looked, as the host of the Rochester Arms had said, 'quite a desolate spot'. It was as still as a church on a week-day: the pattering rain on the forest leaves was the only sound audible in its vicinage.

'Can there be life here?' I asked.

Yes, life of some kind there was; for I heard a movement—that narrow row front door was unclosing, and some shape was about to issue from the grange.

Jane Eyre

T. W. Folley,
author of
*Romantic
Wycoller*

    E. W. Folley, author of *Romantic Wycoller* a keen Brontë lover, showed no doubts about Ferndean Manor when he wrote the following paragraph.

> Brontë worshippers make "Ferndean Manor" a place of pilgrimage . . . Today, lovers of "Jane Eyre" proceed in thousands to look at the ruin. But what a ruin! As soon as one enters the Dene its magic and glamour and romance seize upon the spirit, make us bow the head in silent reverence before blackened stones and confused broken masonry because that spot enshrines for each one the close of a story which holds the world spell-bound. The alembic of Charlotte Brontë's vivid imagination and gift of words made a ruin a haven of happiness. We feel the presence of Jane and her blind husband as we move about the precincts which these mind-created characters inhabited. To thousands of people this consciousness gives assurance that Wycoller Hall is of a truth "Ferndean Manor".

    There is no doubt from the above passage that E. W. Folley also enjoyed a vivid imagination, but we must now consider what solid basis there is for this belief. In 1872 the Brontë publishers Smith and Elder wished to publish illustrated volumes of the Brontë novels and commissioned Edmund Morison Wimperis to prepare the engravings. The artist came to Yorkshire and consulted Ellen Nussey, Charlotte Brontë's friend since their school days together at Roe Head. Ellen gave the location of Ferndean Manor as Kirklees Hall near Huddersfield, and it is interesting to note that she identified the other house in *Jane Eyre*, Thornfield Hall, as her own old home, Rydings, in Birstall.

Although Kirklees appeared in the edition of 1872, when the Haworth edition was published some fifteen years later Ferndean Manor was represented by Wycoller Hall. The Thornton edition of *Jane Eyre* published in 1907 also included a photograph of Wycoller Hall. Herbert F. Wroot, writing for the Brontë Society published *The Persons and Places of Brontë Novels* in 1906. In his remarks about Ferndean Manor H. F. Wroot first tells us how Kirklees Hall was thought to be Ferndean Manor and then adds: "It is now believed that in this identification a mistake was made, and that the original of Ferndean Manor of the novel was Wycoller Hall near Colne". Whatever the case we must remember Phyllis Bentley's warning that "a novelists' locations are sometimes multiple in source".

Did Charlotte and Emily Brontë visit Wycoller Dene? This is the second important question, the answer to which holds great importance to the claim that Wycoller was a haunt of the Brontës. E. W. Folley says: "We must base our creed first upon proximity and the probable. The Haworth and Stanbury moors adjoin those of Wycoller. In their wanders and worships over the moor they were not likely to halt at the slight depression which marks the boundary of Lancashire and Yorkshire. A few more minutes would bring them to the upper reaches of our romantic vale".

E. W. Folley also gives a quotation from *Shirley* which he says "is so exact a description of the Dene that it could only have been written from actual observation".

> *The opposing sides of the glen, approaching each other and becoming clothed with brush-wood and stunted oaks, formed a wooded ravine at the bottom of which ran the mill-stream in broken, unquiet course, struggling with many stones, chafing against rugged banks, fretting with gnarled tree roots, foaming,*

gurgling, battling, as it went. Here, when you have wandered half a mile from the mill, you found a sense of deep solitude; found it in the shade of unmolested trees; received it in the singing of many birds for which that shade made a home. This was no trodden way: the freshness of the wood flowers attested that foot of man seldom pressed them; the abounding wild-roses looked as if they budded, bloomed and faded under the watch of solitude.

Attractive descriptive writing though it is, there is no positive evidence in the text to suggest a real connection with Wycoller—if the imagination is controlled. Wycoller had no mill and rather than an untrodden way a substantial road had passed through the Dene for centuries.

In May 1901 members of the Lancashire and Cheshire Antiquarian Society visited Wycoller to look at the village and the Hall. The following comment was included in the report of the visit: "The ladies were pleased to hear that some old folks had been spoken to who had remembered the Misses Brontë coming down from Barnside; also that Wycoller was the original "Fern Dene" in *Jane Eyre,* and that the Heights above were Wuthering Heights". The Misses Brontë would be Charlotte and Emily but why should they be coming down from Barnside?

In 1850 Charlotte went to stay at Gawthorpe Hall at Padiham in Lancashire, at the invitation of Sir James Kay-Shuttleworth and his wife Lady Janet. Mrs. Gaskell says that "the quiet driving to old ruins and old halls situated amongst older hills and woods—suited the Shuttleworths and did not exhaust Charlotte". So Charlotte Brontë visited old halls and ruins in the Burnley area and there is a strong likelihood that one of them was Wycoller.

It has been considered that it was during Charlotte Brontë's visit to Hathersage in Derbyshire that she absorbed the name Eyre; the Eyre family being lords of the manor and having a tomb there. It is interesting to note that Elizabeth Cunliffe became Elizabeth Eyre by her second marriage and that her children were frequent visitors to Wycoller Hall, showing that there were Eyres much closer at hand than Derbyshire. Betty Eyre lived there much longer than her brother Thomas, but it was Thomas Eyre who came very near to inheriting Wycoller Hall and the estates. Perhaps Thomas's children and grandchildren came back to Wycoller from time to time in the nineteenth century to see the old Hall that might well have been their inheritance. Few people have known of the Eyre connection with Wycoller Hall but perhaps it had not escaped Charlotte Brontë.

If we are to believe Mrs Gaskell, Charlotte certainly knew of the cock-fighting squire who had lived only a few miles from Haworth. She may also have known that in his later years he only visited Wycoller in the shooting season. In *Jane Eyre* we are told that of all the rooms at Ferndean only two or three remained furnished for the use of the squire when he went there to shoot.

In the final analysis it must be a question of faith. To those holding the faith there is no doubt that it was here at Wycoller Hall, after the death of his poor mad wife, Rochester retired to lick his wounds. Here he was sought by Jane Eyre and by her nursed back to sight and health.

The embellishment of Wycoller legends is due more than anything else to the work of novelist Halliwell Sutcliffe. Although he lived at Rylstone in Yorkshire, he made Wycoller and the moorland around it the source of several of his novels and frequently came to stay in the area, often lodging with the Biker family in Laneshawbridge. A quiet man he spent his time tramping the moors alone to learn the traditions and legends of the area and to take in the spirit of the countryside which so fascinated him.

Halliwell Sutcliffe

Mistress Barbara Cunliffe, Through Sorrow's Gates and *Lonesome Heights* are all set in the area, their heroes and heroines frequently visiting the Herders Inn and wandering in the Wycoller valley below. It was in *Mistress Barbara Cunliffe* that he introduced the character Simon Cunliffe, a character frequently promoted to fact. It is only recently that a popular writer in a national magazine told the story of Squire Simon Cunliffe of Wycoller Hall and the legends which had sprung up around him.

He loved to recount the legend and the ghost story and the Ghostly Hunting Squire, the Sorrowful Woman, Guytrash, Barguest and the Heath Brown Man appear with regularity throughout his novels.

> ... he had felt the eerie glamour of the Dene below, whose every wrinkle, every bush and warren, was known to him. And the old Hall there, with its roystering, luckless line of Cunliffes – had he not felt his boy's heart fail him, as he wandered in and out among the ruins, and hearkened for the Ghostly Huntsman, and heard the legendary folk come back to life again and rustle up and down the oaken stairs. *Mistress Barbara Cunliffe.*

> *... when the moor ran red with blood feuds, when Barguest and the Sorrowful Woman, gnomes and the Heath Brown Man, had fixed this spell upon the land and made the men, who in the daytime fought staunchly against mortal foes, fall to trembling at gloaming-tide for dread of ghostly visitations.*
>
> *Through Sorrow's Gates.*

Wycoller Hall was often featured in his writing and his characters frequently find themselves wandering in its ruins and being subjected to its mysterious influences. In *Through Sorrow's Gates* Ned o' Bracken Clough, after a meal at the Herders Inn, came down into Wycoller to look for his friends. It was already growing dark as he entered the village from the Dene.

"A main, a main! My bird against yours for a sovereign", were the first words he heard.

Now, a cock-fight was no new thing to Ned, but what in another place would have seemed usual enough was the cause of cringing dread to the man tonight . . . Ned o' Bracken Clough recalled the tale of another of the wild Cunliffe breed—how the Squire of that day lay a-dying, and called for a pair of fighting cocks, and died cheering on the winning bird. How if his ghost had come back to old scenes, old occupations? The Hall had been untenanted and shunned for years; none would enter it for a cock-fight now, unless he was mad drunk or disembodied.

Again the shouts came from the upper chamber and Ned, drawn by an awful fascination, passed through the gate, and in between the straight, tall hollies that guarded each side of the doorway, and up the worn stone stairs, He moved more slowly and reluctantly with every step, and yet he felt compelled to mount. At last he stood upon the landing, in front of the closed door from under which the light was stealing. With a sudden effort he pushed the door wide open and looked within, holding his breath for dread of the unknown whose secret he must learn.

What he saw was a company of twelve, surrounding the bodies of two fighting-cocks, one bird was dead, the other dying in its hour of victory. The men's faces were fierce and eager, and they were shouting wildly or cursing, according to the wagers they had made. Squat, round-bellied bottles stood on the window seat, and in the neck of such bottles as were empty were thrust the candles which had guided Ned into the midst of this harsh revelry.

. . . Now the candle flames, and now the lightning, revealed the dead bodies of the fighting cocks, the bottles, some upright, some lying on their sides; revealed the wild faces of the revelers; revealed last of all the dark stain upon the floor which was connected with one of the far off Cunliffe tragedies . . . A roar of thunder, and then a crash of masonry as the chimney stack fell inward, filling the chamber with the odour of damp earth and soot. The wind got up again and howled; and then again it shrieked in agony, and swept through the hall door, left open by Ned on his first coming, and ran like a mad thing up the stair. The Squireen's mug fell to the floor. "By the Heart, its the Riding Squire himself!" he yelled, and raced wildly for the stair.

Halliwell Sutcliffe's stories are much concerned with farmers and peasants, their struggle against the moorland to intake good land from waste; their struggle against the weather in winter, and their struggle against fear of the unknown. The characters are fated to struggle; they are portrayed growing strong through hard work; enriched by suffering and comforted and saved through love. Although the stories are homely, and by modern standards lacking polish and excitement, they are well worth the attention of those who have a feeling for the area.

People and Work

Wycoller families

The first recorded families in Wycoller—Hartley, Foulds and Emmott—were the families who farmed the vaccaries along with their neighbours. As the population grew after the disafforestation, new family names appear in the village such as Hargreaves, Driver and Cunliffe. By 1660 there were thirteen families settled in the valley's farmsteads and their names are recorded in the Poll Tax of that year. Wycoller being in the Chapelry of Colne the baptisms, marriages and burials of Wycoller folk are to be found registered at Colne. The registers began in 1599 and from these we can get a rough estimate of the population as well as see the names of the families coming into the area. Between 1630 and 1660 around sixty Wycoller children were baptised at Colne Parish Church and from 1730 to 1760 the figure was around one hundred and ten. During that century the number of births in the village had almost doubled. The population of around forty in the Tudor period had increased to about seventy five by 1660 and by 1760 was in the region of one hundred and eighty. The names of the families who came into Wycoller between 1700 and 1760 included Bradley, Spencer, Pearson, Mitchell, Ellis, Cowgill, Stell, Binns, Greenwood, Blakey, Kay, Shackleton, Rycroft, Halstead, Pickles, Hindle, Foster, Blackburn, Edmondson, Harrison, Laycock, Eyre, Whitehead, Catlow, Holgate, Crabtree, Tattersall, Preston and Stephenson. By the seventeen sixties the population had grown far in excess of what the valley could support by farming. By this time weaving had become more than just a secondary occupation for many families who made their livings solely from the produce of their handlooms.

Until the seventeenth century the sole place of worship for Wycoller folk was the Parish Church in Colne and that was the centre of all their religious activities and services. In the seventeenth century the Quakers began to challenge the Established Church in the Wycoller area, but during the eighteenth century a wider challenge came from the Inghamites and the Methodists. Benjamin Ingham was born at Ossett, near Dewsbury in Yorkshire, in 1712 and was ordained in 1735. He broke away from the Established Church around 1740 and formed his own religious groups in

Inghamites

Yorkshire. William Batty was one of his main preachers, and it was from his church history that we learn how Wycoller was the first place in Lancashire visited by Benjamin Ingham.

> *As Benjamin Ingham returned home he met Joseph Gawkroger between Tingley and Thorpe, who told him several people wanted to hear him about Colne in Lancashire, asking him when he would come and he would give notice; this was Feby 15, 1742. Benjamin Ingham then behoved it was a call from the Lord to go into Lancashire having an impression on his heart; and a few days after it was made more clear to him so that he went forward on Feby 23rd he came ye first night to Haworth and lodg'd at the Clerks house whereby he became acquainted with Mr. Grimshaw ye minister of ye church who invited him to preach in his parish. On Thurs Feby 29 he went to Wycoller to Mr Pearson's and then to Colne ... At Wycoller he heard that some people used to meet together in Colne Church Yard he enquired of the Landlady of the Red Lyon where he lodg'd at what house they met.*

Benjamin Ingham preached at Wycoller on his second visit to Lancashire on 23 March 1742, and came back many times in the years that followed. The Inghamites gained considerable influence in Trawden Forest and erected a Chapel at Winewall in 1752. Many Wycoller people attended Winewall Chapel, and a few Wycoller children were baptised by Benjamin Ingham and William Batty. In the fifty years between 1770 and 1820 over a hundred and thirty inhabitants of Wycoller were buried in the Inghamite Chapel burial ground at Winewall.

Another eighteenth-century preacher who knew Wycoller well was William Darney, a lay preacher under John Wesley. Wycoller was the scene of William Darney's operations as is shown by one verse of a long rhyme written by him. *William Darney*

> *To Chipping and to Wycoller*
> *We go each fortnight day:*
> *I wish we could see fruit appear;*
> *For that we still do pray.*

In the early days many people had done their own carding, spinning and weaving as a family operation but soon wealthier yeomen began to have their wool spun by poorer neighbours, and thus the clothier came into existence. The term clothier seems to have been a wide-ranging one including both the yeoman farmer who sold a few pieces in the local markets as well as the wealthy *Weaving*

Colne Cloth Hall opened in December, 1775

manufacturer who employed scores of men working in their own homes and who sold his cloth throughout the world. The first clothier noted in Wycoller was William Hargreaves who died in 1598. As no inventory of his goods has survived we have no record of his weaving equipment and stock of cloth. However, his will does mention debts owing to him by several citizens of London. The first Robert Stork owed him £100, the second Henry Flint owed him £9. 13s. 4d. and the third John Turner owed him £80. It appears, then, that William Hargreaves was a clothier on a considerable scale who disposed of his cloth not only in the local markets but also in London. It is likely that William sent cloth to be sold in the weekly London cloth markets and the yearly cloth fair held on St. Bartholomew's day. The cloth would be sent to London by pack-horse carrier and once there it would be received by his London agents or cloth factors—the three citizens of London mentioned in his will Robert Stork, Henry Flint and John Turner were most probably his London agents. The will of John Whitaker, a Wycoller clothier who died in 1671, shows him to have been a substantial yeoman farmer with considerable cattle and sheep as well as his weaving equipment and cloth.

When the Colne Cloth Hall was erected in 1775 both Henry Owen Cunliffe and Richard Foulds, a Wycoller 'piecemaker', were among the shareholders. The Cloth Hall was erected as a market both for

132

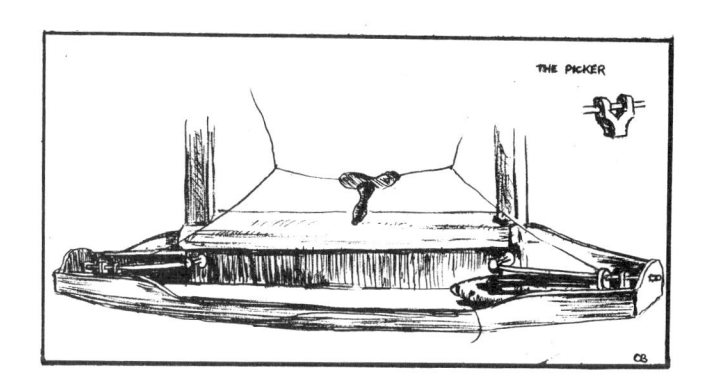

Kay's Flying Shuttle

clothiers and independent weavers. Statistics for the production of worsted cloth during the year 1781 are as follows:

	Inhabitants	No. of Pieces	Value
Colne and Township	2,757	13,534	£16,994
Great Marsden	993	8,079	£10,518
Little Marsden	772	5,940	£ 7,987
Trawden	1,120	7,578	£10,843
Barrowford	1,006	4,793	£ 5,944
Foulridge	615	2,919	£ 3,112
Total for Colne Chapelry	7,263	42,843	£54,900
Total for Burnley Chapelry	5,574	19,991	£32,166

Evidence from probate inventories shows that many Tudor and Stuart families who were involved in cloth making frequently had cards for carding, combs for woolcombing, wheels for spinning and looms for weaving. It is obvious that some were involved in the complete process from clipping the wool from the sheep's back to stretching it on the tenting frames that stood in Tenter Field. However, by the late eighteenth century there were few people in Wycoller employed in any other branch of cloth making other than weaving. John Kay had invented the flying shuttle in 1733 and some thirty years later, when its use had become more widespread, it had greatly speeded up the process of woollen weaving. To keep pace with the woollen weavers, spinning methods had to be improved and work became more specialised.

Woolcombers

There were four woolcombers in Wycoller between 1790 and 1810, but none remained a few years afterwards. The four were Thomas Edmondson, John Heap, William Riley and Richard Riley of Height Laithe. It is probably a coincidence that there were four of them but four is a significant number in woolcombing. The main tools of the woolcomber were two large combs and a stove or pot in which to heat them. The pot usually had slots for four combs to be heated at once, and hence the term "pot of four". Wycoller's woolcombers were preparing wool for the making of worsted cloth, for Wycoller specialised in worsted weaving. This concentration on worsted materials grew from about 1700 until by 1780 it was almost the only cloth woven in Wycoller. Ordinary woollen cloth was woven from yarn spun from carded wool. Hand cards teased the wool and caused the wool fibres to lock into each other. The cloth was treated in the fulling stocks to mat the warp and weft together and produce a smooth cloth. Worsted cloth, however, was woven from smoother, thinner and stronger yarn—yarn which had been spun from combed wool. The long fibres drawn out in the combing process produced spun yarns of extra strength. Worsted cloth was strong and, having a closer weave, it did not need to be fulled.

Hand wool combing in the late eighteenth century. Courtesy of the Bankfield Museum, Halifax

By the early years of the nineteenth century it appears that all the preparatory work on wool and yarn was done outside Wycoller. The yarn was brought to the handloom weavers by the clothier who later collected the complete pieces at a local centre. Wycoller's handloom weavers were paid by the piece, that is paid a fixed price for every length of cloth they wove. There were few, if any, independent weavers; the majority wove the clothiers yarn into the clothiers cloth and were paid a wage for doing so.

In Wycoller there were few specially-built cottages for handloom weavers, and looms were placed in every conceivable room. Some had looms in the kitchen and others in the living room while a common site was the bedroom. We know that Timmy Feather of Stanbury, the last handloom weaver in the Lancashire-Yorkshire border area, kept his handloom in his bedroom. Born in 1825 he continued handloom weaving until shortly before his death in 1910.

> *There stood upstairs an old handloom,*
> *Close by my parents' bed,*
> *A cuckoo clock with flowered face,*
> *And heavy weight of lead;*
> *The fifty-jenny—my mother span,*
> *The skips and slubbing creel,*
> *The "chovin dish," the sizing pan,*
> *The twelve-staved bobbin wheel.*
>
> *A. Wrigley*

Timmy Feather's handloom now at Cliffe Castle Museum, Keighley

The population of Wycoller reached its height about 1820 when some 350 people lived there. In 1841 the population was 315 and there were a few empty houses. By 1851 the population had dropped to 231 but Wycoller was still a thriving village. Wycoller, standing as it does exactly on the border of East Lancashire and West Yorkshire, was influenced by the textile trade of both counties. By 1841 some 28 of Wycoller's handloom weavers were weaving cotton, Lancashire's chief textile. The remainder were still weaving worsted cloth. It was the introduction of the power loom into the Lancashire cotton trade which by 1851 had drawn out Wycoller's cotton handloom weavers almost to a man. This was the cause of a drop in population from 315 to 231.

Population in 1851   By 1851 Wycoller's 68 handloom weavers were weaving worsted cloth with the exception of a few satin and 'Delaine' weavers. The impression has been given by previous writers on Wycoller that handloom weavers were a dying breed in the early nineteenth century—the period when they probably reached their peak, in spite of the fact that the Industrial Revolution was creeping up on them. It is also often thought that those handloom weavers who were left around 1850 were a few old men working out their time in the

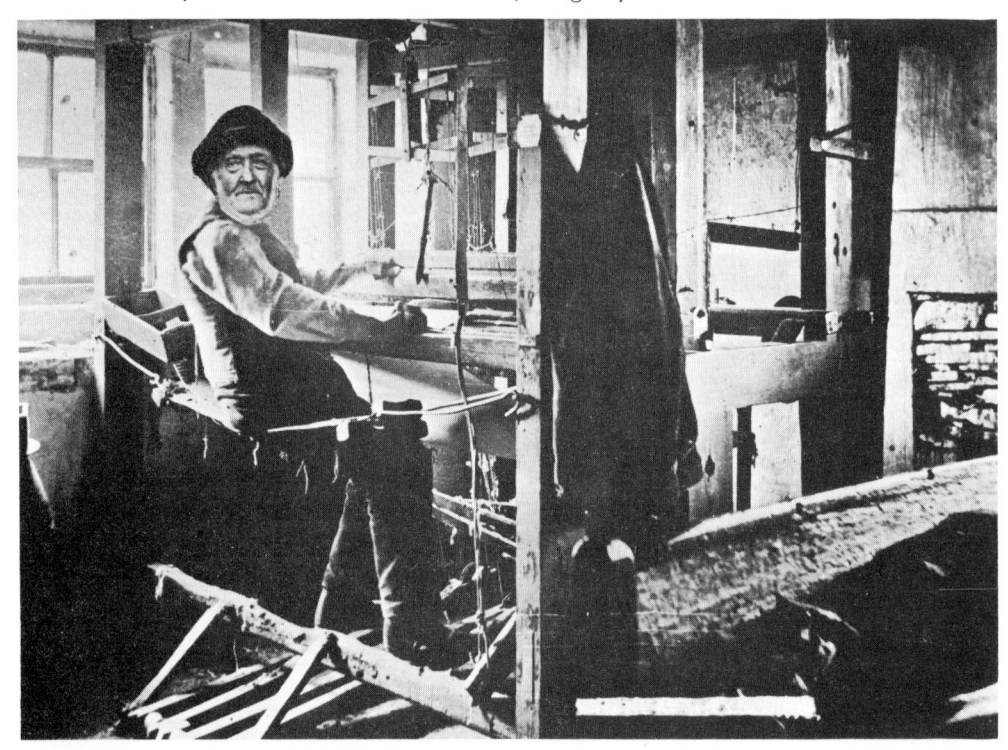

Timmy Feather at his handloom in the bedroom of his Stanbury cottage
Courtesy of the Cliffe Castle Museum, Keighley

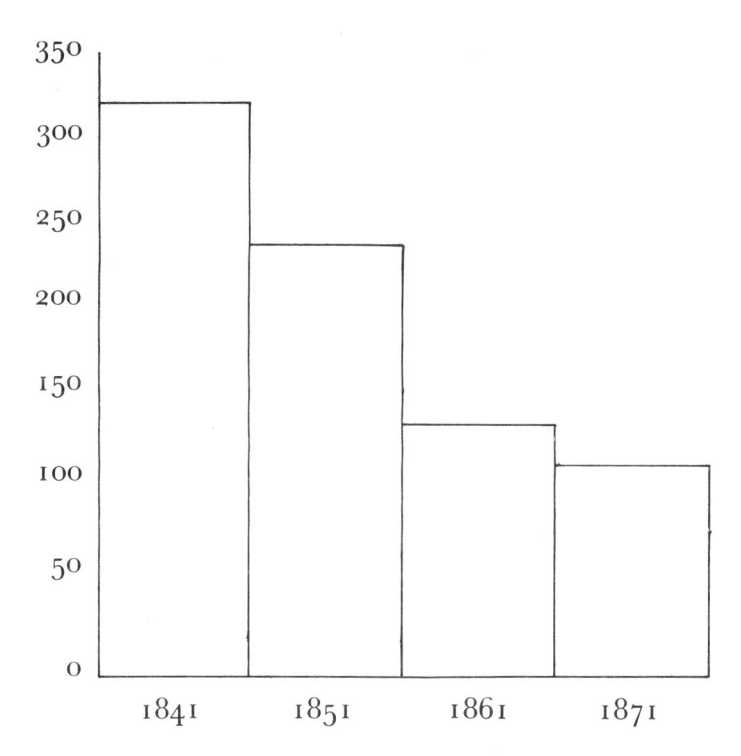

Population Fall 1841-1871 Due to Extinction of Handloom Weaving

only trade they knew. The facts prove otherwise. A surprise to some will be that 41% of Wycoller's handloom weavers were female, 25% being girls from the age of 12 to 20 years. Of the male weavers a third were under the age of 20. The rest of Wycoller's working population was composed of 21 farmers, 12 agricultural labourers, 2 dairy maids, a gamekeeper, a woodturner and a pedlar. The rest of the population were children, retired persons and two landed proprietors.

The population of Wycoller in 1851 was a healthy one from a demographic point of view. Its population of 231 had a broad base of 85 children under 15 years of age which, allowing for the high infant mortality rate of Victorian times, still promised a strong future generation for the village. There was a good working population between the ages of 20 and 55 years. There were only 11 inhabitants over the age of 65 which indicates that few survived to old age. Wycoller's population, however, was not to thrive as there was no mill in the valley, and for many the only alternative to handloom

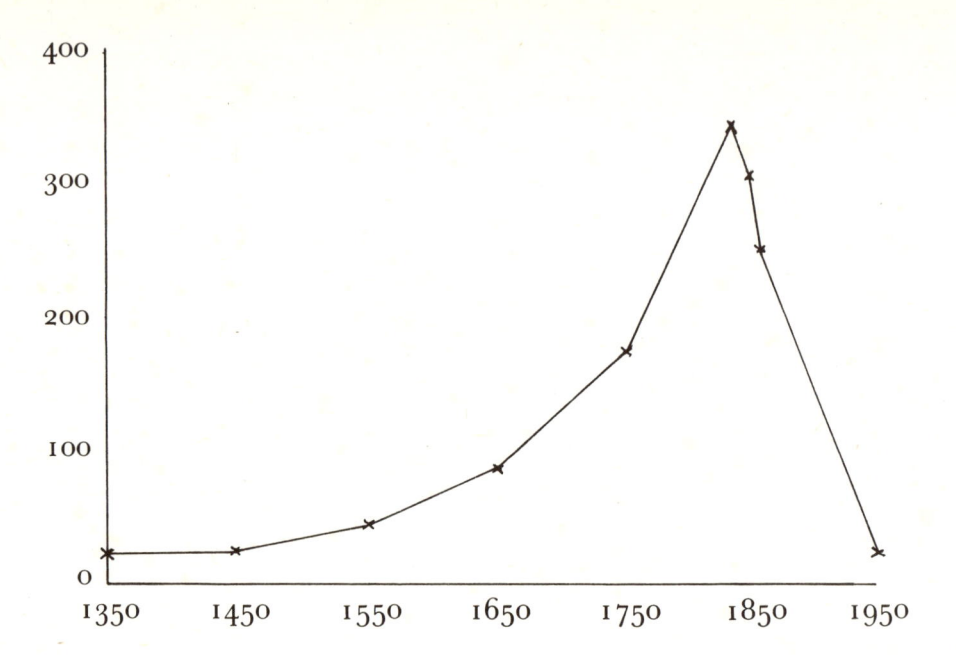

Approximate Population of Wycoller over the Centuries.

weaving was to leave the village or walk to work in the mills of the neighbouring towns of Trawden and Colne. By 1861 the population had dropped to 126 and by 1871 it was 107. By the eighteen seventies the Industrial Revolution had finally tightened its stranglehold on Wycoller. The census return of 1871 shows that Henry Hindle, his son Hartley and his daughter Elizabeth were the last surviving worsted handloom weavers. The population of 107 was now mainly composed of farmers and farm labourers. Wycoller had gone back to concern itself with the land.

Farms, Fields and Cottages

On the slopes of the Wycoller valley, out of the village, yet within the Wycoller boundaries stand many old farms with such interesting names as Height Laithe, Foster Leap, Parson Lee, Raven Rock and Key Stiles. Most of these farms have remained occupied even though the village became almost deserted, and it will be worthwhile to look at some of the buildings and recount a little of their past.

High above the village of Wycoller on the Laneshawbridge Haworth road stands Height Laithe sheltered by a clump of trees. *Height Laithe*

Height Laithe Farm

Foster Leap

It has been said to be the Wuthering Heights of Emily Brontë's novel and though this is unlikely its position and name allow it some claim. Height Laithe has stood at least from 1660 when the Riley family lived there; a branch of the Riley family still occupied the house well over a century later. During the nineteenth century the Wallbank family were in residence and farmed the sixty acres of pasture and meadow and two hundred acres of common.

This farm is the holder of one of Wycoller's more intriguing farm names, and several local fields and the nearby gritstone rocks bear the same name. Existing from the seventeenth century, this is

Foster Leap Farm

one of the farms which Henry Owen Cunliffe added to the Cunliffe estate by a surrender of 19 May 1797 "in consideration of £981 unto the said John Whitham paid by Henry Owen Cunliffe of Wycoller Hall, Lancs Esq. in full for the absolute purchase of tenements and hereditaments". At that time there were four cottages adjoining or near Foster Leap. The farm included "one close called Robinson Close and liberty to a place called Fence as had been usually occupied and enjoyed with the aforesaid premises, with a part of the limestone scar lying in Smithy Clough".

The Herders Inn lies at the edge of wild and desolate moorland full of romance and legend. This solitary inn, officially the Oldham Arms, was the Herders House long before it became an inn around 1860. Originally it is said that two herders cottages stood on the site. The present building which has a pleasant eighteenth century facade onto the Haworth road featured in several of Halliwell Sutcliffe's novels including *Through Sorrow's Gates*, *Mistress Barbara Cunliffe* and *Ricroft of Withens*. In the nineteenth century before it became an inn the families who lived there were involved in handloom weaving, for example the Laycock family in 1841 and the Hopkinson family in 1851. The first publican was John Lund whose occupation was given as Ale Retailer in 1861. The second publican was Thomas Feather who came from Keighley and lived with his wife Maria and several children. Little is known about the inn at that time but one writer wrote about it in 1923. "Quite innocent of all modern innovation are its clean white wooden benches, and its tidily sanded floor, while

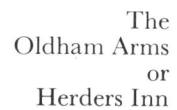

The Herders Inn

The Oldham Arms or Herders Inn

Upper and Lower Key Stiles

its fare is just as characteristically plain and hearty. A basin of broth, with its toothsome dumpling, for the winter time; the pop and beer 'smiler' for the dog days".

Key Stiles   Not far from the Herders, below the brow of the hill and sheltered by rocks stands Key Stiles. This farm was named Castille on the 1844 Tithe Award Map and the spelling has varied through the years from Kay Stile to Key Steel and Key Steal. Perhaps its name originated from the Kay family. In 1851 the farm was composed of sixteen acres and thirty four acres of common. Mark Foulds was the farmer then and his two lodgers were employed in handloom weaving.

A field length from Key Stiles, Woodcock Hall stood alongside the Laneshawbridge to Haworth road. Once again it was a handloom weavers house although it was later said to have been an inn known as the Old Cock. The building has long since been demolished

142

Evening view from Combe Hill Cross

the only sign of its existence being a flat patch of ground near the gateway leading down to Key Stiles. Further along the Haworth road, yet still within the Wycoller boundary, stand Near Cross and Far Cross Farms. Far Cross is frequently referred to as Camel Cross and Combe Hill Cross. The farms take their names from Combe Hill Cross, the old highway cross, the remains of which still stand overlooking the farms.

Combe Hill Cross

Combes House stands in the fields below Near Cross. A long farm composed of house and barn its stonework shows the signs of many centuries. Derelict for many years there is now a possibility of its renovation. This farm has also been known as Roger Laithe possibly due to Roger Robinson who farmed its twenty six acres for many years in the nineteenth century. Combes House was part of Henry Owen Cunliffe's estate and was sold to Richard Hartley in 1859 for £550.

Combes House

143

Smithy Clough or Smithy Cote lies in a scarred valley

Smithy Clough   In Smithy Clough below these farms lie the remains of Smithy Clough or Smithy Cote Farm. This tiny farm of only six acres has stood a ruin for around a hundred years but the steps leading upstairs can still be seen cut deep by the generations of inhabitants. In 1851 William Wallbank lived here with his wife Susan and sons John and William. William farmed the puny six acres while his sons augmented the family income with the produce of their handlooms. It is a lonely spot offering few comforts. The Wallbanks were probably the last family to live there; in 1871 it was empty and since that date it has been home only to sheep. The fields of Smithy

Parson Lee Farm

Clough and nearby Combes House were added to Near Cross Farm.

Smithy Clough was the site of limestone scars which were quarried over several centuries. Rights to the scars are mentioned in the deeds of Combes House and the other local farms during the eighteenth and nineteenth centuries. The lime was burnt in local lime kilns and was used both for fertilizing the fields and for use in building. The remains of the excavations in Smithy Clough are frequently referred to as the "Hilly Holes".

Further down Smithy Clough towards the village stands Parson Lee Farm. Its old barn could well have been the original farm building while the newer buildings date from the eighteenth century. In 1851 it was a farm of fifty three acres and two hundred acres of common. There is some unusual masonry on the gable of the old barn. The building has an ecclesiastical crocketed finial below which are drip stones and an owl stone, said to be a hole through which owls were allowed access into the barn to kill rats and mice.

Parson Lee

145

The Preston family lived at Parson Lee around 1800. Thomas Preston was both a farmer and tanner. By 1851 the farm was owned by the Robinsons but the Census Return of that year includes "William Preston Vagrant". William Preston was born at Parson Lee in 1801 and he was probably still clinging to the place of his birth and remembering better times when his father was master there.

Dean House   From Parson Lee a footpath crosses to Dean House which was known as Kippax Tenement during the latter part of the seventeenth century and became Dean House in the early eighteenth. John Kippax and his wife Allison lived there in 1660 although the farmhouse has since been rebuilt and at the present time is uninhabited. On the first Ordnance Survey map of 1848 the farm is titled Lower Parson Lee. The fields dip steeply from Dean House down into Turn Hole Clough and on the other side at the top of Great Meadow stands Bank House, a farm which at the present time

Bank House   is both uninhabited and dilapidated. A deed dated May 1690 mentions a house and barn, lately erected at the Banks in the Dean in Wycoller. It is possible that this was the older building at Bank House which at that time was being sold by John Foulds of Wycoller to William Lowcock. The barn attached to the more recent farmhouse has a date-stone inscribed J.AH. 1831.

Copy House   Copy House was a farm of ninety acres in the last century and for many years Robert Tillotson lived there. Three of his children were

Copy House and Crank above it

Two-headed calf born at Copy House in 1923

worsted handloom weavers. The poor land was not sufficient to maintain the family so the wages of the handloom weavers were vital. It was at Copy House that a two-headed calf was born in May 1923. T. M. Bainbridge was the farmer at the time and people from a wide area came to view this freak of nature. For a few weeks the calf was active and well but it did eventually die. The calf's head was divided into two parts, which were practically the same. There was only one neck but the calf had four eyes and two mouths.

Above Copy House stands Raven Rock known for the pulpit stiles which stand in its fields. These two stiles built off the ground are formed like a church pulpit with steps leading up to them. The remaining two farms before we look at the village itself are Bracken Hills and Oak House. The eighteenth century farm of Bracken Hills had thirty one acres of land in 1871 when Joseph Sunderland farmed there. In earlier days its inhabitants were involved in handloom weaving. Oak House was named Hawks House on some early maps and is so named in several deeds. Whether the origin of the name is Oak or Hawk is impossible to say.

Thistleholme Cottage late Dene Cottage

A close study of the farms in the village of Wycoller itself gives rise to many problems for the historian. The problems begin as soon as we look at Lowlands Farm, the first in the village, for this farm did not exist in 1844. The present farmhouse was then cottage property and the fields were attached to the farm known as Bents or Thistleholme. About the year 1900 when Thistleholme Farm lost its land the farmhouse became Dene Cottage—now it is once again Thistleholme.

In Wycoller farm names changed with regularity but to complicate things further, not only were different names applied to the same building, but also the same name was applied to different buildings. Both these variations can be seen when we consider Pearson's Farm. What this farm was called when it was erected is not known but since then it has been Wilkinson's Farm, Pearson's Farm, Laithe Hills Farm and Wycoller Farm. Before we reveal the facts we must dispel fancy. E. W. Folley writes in *Romantic Wycoller*.

Pearson's Farm

This house erroneously called "Laithe Hills," is "Pearson's Farm": it has the architecture of the Hall the first owner of which was Piers Hartley. If a son had lived at the fine house we are describing, it would naturally be "Piers' son's house." (Pearson is fairly common in some districts) Colne Corporation own fifty acres of land known as "Pearson's Farm," so let that name stand and commemorate Piers' son for ever.

Apart from the fact that it is highly unlikely that Piers Hartley built Wycoller Hall it is certain that Pearson's Farm does not commemorate any son of Piers. Pearson's Farm was so named because the Pearson family lived there during the eighteenth century. Henry Pearson died at Wycoller in 1789 and the fact that his daughter had married Edmund Wilkinson of Broad Bank in Briercliffe gave rise to the farm being known as Wilkinson's.

Colne Corporation later gave the farm the name of Laithe Hills, which surely they had every right to do. The farm continued to be known as Laithe Hills until 1943 when the Water Department decided to change its name to Wycoller Farm. The decision was explained in the Water Department's report: "On the late tenant leaving Wycoller Farm in 1943 this and the Laithe Hill farm were merged into one farm under the tenancy of Mr. W. Bracewell, the tenant of the latter farm, the whole to be named the Wycoller Farm in order to preserve the village association, and the original Wycoller farm house to be called Wycoller Cottage". So Wycoller Cottage or Emmott's Cottage was formerly Wycoller Farm. Now, however, we must consider it as a cottage. This is the problem in Wycoller where buildings have been cottage, farm, barn, and even hall in their long history.

Wycoller Hall Wycoller Hall itself is such a building or complex of buildings. It is unlikely that the ruins now known as Wycoller Hall were ever

Wycoller Hall c. 1890

one dwelling. Here is the ruin of a complex of dwellings, dwellings that grew over the years almost organically. Wycoller Hall is unlikely to have been built in 1550, 1560, 1590, 1593 or 1596, as in spite of such dates being given in several publications there is little if any evidence to substantiate them. So much incorrect information has been written about this Hall that it is difficult to know where to begin. It could almost be said that everything previously written in *Romantic Wycoller, Calderdale, The Annals of Trawden Forest* and countless other articles can be completely discounted. Fred Bannister writes that "Piers Hartley settled in Wycoller previous to 1507 and built Wycoller in 1550". Written in 1922 this unsubstantiated information has frequently been repeated. From 1500 to 1625 there were several Peter Hartley's living in Wycoller, often three or more being alive at the same time. There is no evidence that Peter Hartley built Wycoller Hall but as most of the inhabitants were surnamed Hartley and as many were christened Peter there must be a strong chance of it being true. The well known arched fire-place is not Tudor, the high mullioned windows are neither Tudor nor Stuart, the Hall was never one dwelling and it was not abandoned after the death of Henry Owen Cunliffe.

Worn steps behind the fire-place in the Hall

The building first erected on the site of the Hall was likely to have been a timber building. The timber building would almost probably have been replaced in the late sixteenth or early seventeenth century by a stone built farmhouse. We know from the will of John Pearson that the south-east wing was three storied in 1695. The north end of the Hall was the site of cottages from the seventeenth to the late nineteenth century. In 1710 Percy Shackleton's address was given in the parish registers as Wycoller North Hall and we shall see later that several cottages existed there around 1850.

In 1774 Henry Owen Cunliffe carried out alterations to make his home at Wycoller less of a farmhouse and more of a hall. He built the handsome fire-place, had a new bank of high mullioned windows set in the south-west side, had new windows built in the south-east end, and had a new porch erected. At the same time as the fire-place was built the keyhole shaped opening was also constructed. This small storage place has given rise to a great deal of speculation. Some have considered it a well, others a storage place for guns and powder. E. W. Folley says that it was for storing logs whilst others are equally certain that it was a wig cupboard. Clearing out the rubbish proved that it was not a well but apart from that the question is still open.

Puzzling niche—
a storage place
for guns,
a wig cupboard,
a log store?

In many publications concerning Wycoller there are paintings purporting to show Christmas festivities at Wycoller Hall in the Stuart period. The painting in *Romantic Wycoller* is entitled, "John Cunliffe at Wycoller Hall. Christmas Festivities 1660." A copy of the same picture in *Wycoller Country Park* is captioned "Christmas in 1650—hey days at Wycoller". These pictures are obvious fabrications produced in the nineteenth century as the fire-place and new door portrayed in the pictures did not exist until 1774.

The porch of Wycoller Hall was removed to Trawden where it was built onto a house in Church Street. Fred Bannister tells the story in *The Annals of Trawden Forest*. *Wycoller Hall porch*

> *Scar Top Mill, or Shipley, was built by my grandfather, John Bannister, while he was the corn miller . . . The New End of this mill, an enlargement, was built entirely of material from Wycoller Hall, which was then being dismantled and sold piece-meal. At the same time he bought and removed the "haunted chamber" and the front doorway and entrance hall, and erected them behind his own house, where they still remain unchanged . . . The outer gate pillars were also removed and placed in Church Street at the entrance of the mill road. They were massive square columns composed of hewn rectangular blocks surmounted by pyramidal capitals, and stood about nine feet high. These structures were originally almost exactly opposite the end of the stone foot bridge by which Wycoller Hall ruins are approached.*

The porch was later promised to the Friends of Wycoller and but for the lack of funds would have been re-erected at the Hall. However, it has once again been removed, this time to Ball House at Foulridge.

Wycoller Hall was dispersed both in fact and fiction. The porch and other ornamental stone went to Trawden, some of its flagstones and steps are said to have been used in walls at Trawden and a supposed stone bath is said to have been dragged to Floyt Bridge Farm in Nelson by seventeen ponies. As the stone trough is too big either to have gone in or out of Wycoller Hall the story is most unlikely. A second story has the bath from the Hall at Coldwell Farm. Wycoller Hall has been dispersed and despoiled yet fated to remain a ruin—like a ghost to haunt the valley.

The old barn or coach house in the Hall grounds is another interesting but puzzling building. Its timbers show signs of being previously used in other buildings and there are many unusual *Coach House*

153

154

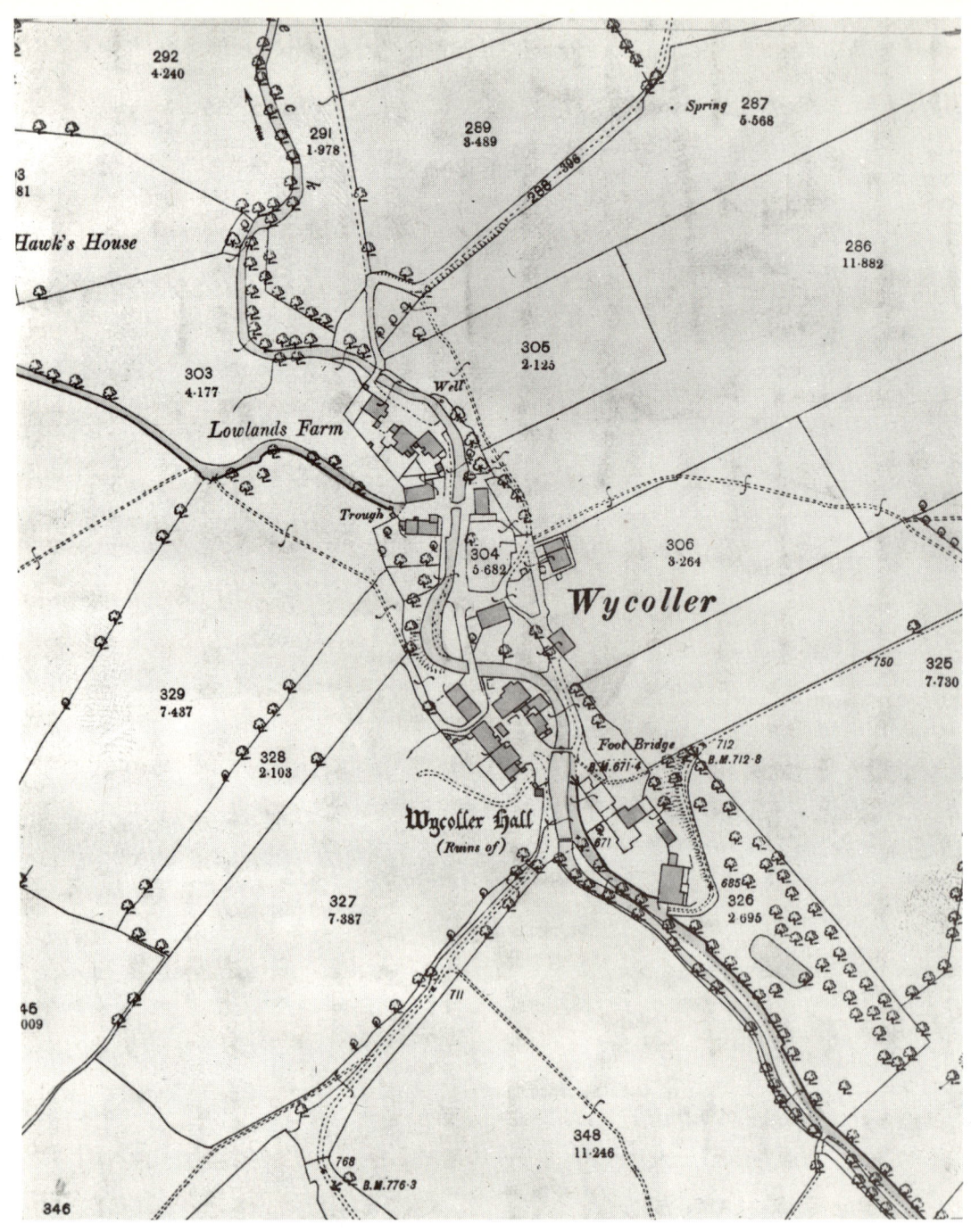

The village
from the first
large scale
Ordnance Survey
Map of 1893
Courtesy
of the
Ordnance
Survey

Interior of the old coach house

sections of walling which are difficult to explain. As the Ordnance Survey map of 1893 shows, the barn had a cottage attached to the north end. The arch stoned doorways were used when the building was used as a coach house, but later when it was used for cattle and hay storage the doorways were walled up.

Cottages

A hundred and fifty years ago when the population of Wycoller was over three hundred there were many more cottages than those that remain today. Some have been demolished in living memory but many others have gone and been forgotten. The first large-scale Ordnance Survey map published in 1893 shows the state of the village around a hundred years ago.

Laithe Hills Cottage

As the road from Trawden enters the village it passes Laithe Hills Cottage on the right. This cottage was long a ruin and its demolition was approved by Trawden Council many years ago. Following the pressures of the Wycoller Preservation Committee this cottage was one of two sold by the Water Board in 1965. The cottage was sold to R. J. Wood of Bury for £150. Renovations were

Laithe Hills Cottage

carried out and the next time the cottage changed hands the price was said to have been over £14,000. To remember the condition of the cottage in 1965 is to realise what a remarkable change has been made both to the house and the gardens.

Across the road stood the old Laithe Hills barn which was demolished in 1968. This was a fine structure reduced to ruin by age and lack of repair. Just over the bridge at Laithe Hills stood three cottages. Looking over the wall today there is no trace to show that these cottages ever existed. Luckily photographs have survived and we can see the cottages that were once the home of Wycoller folk. On Pepper Hill behind these cottages stood a tenement block of about six dwellings. Their foundations can still be traced in the grass but it is difficult to believe that six dwellings once stood on this small spot. The block was almost fully inhabited in 1851 when five families comprised of about twenty persons

Pepper Hill Cottages

Laithe Hills Barn

lived there. By 1871 William Varley aged 79 years, his sons John and William and grand-daughter Hannah, occupied one house and the rest were uninhabited. The block must have been demolished before the turn of the century as no living person remembers the building and no photographs of it have been discovered. A further cottage stood in a croft immediately below but this has also long since disappeared.

The next cottages are those opposite Wycoller House. There were several cottages here, one of which was used as a Methodist Chapel for many years. Wycoller House is a building frequently referred to as a fine seventeenth century house. The house has been examined by architects and historians and some have noted that there are signs of changes. Richard Hartley lived in this house and on his death in 1892 his daughter Susanah Hartley had to supply details to the Inland Revenue. The Inland Revenue account includes "Three cottages thrown together by the late Richard Hartley and used by him as a Dwelling House".

So Wycoller House is a Victorian reconstruction composed of three old cottages and the reconstruction took place about 1860. At the same time the mock mullioned windows were added to match, or nearly to match, the older ones and the stone roof flags were removed and replaced with slate. This house has also been the

Wycoller House

home of Fred Smith, John Mitchell and Frank and Nesta Dewhurst who lived there until 1957. The house was bought by schoolmaster Alan Gates for £450 and he in turn sold it to Foster Willan for £700 in 1963. The property included a cottage opposite the house and a small croft. Foster Willan was reported as selling the house, still a shell, for £10,000 and it was later advertised for £12,000, which must be a record for a derelict house without windows, drains, septic tank or power. When Nigel Taylor bought the house in January 1974 the story was reported in the *Daily Express*. The historical account said that the village was deserted and had been deserted for almost two hundred years—statements which were not only untrue but quite ridiculous. This building has been much spoiled in recent years by heavy sand blasting and by being strap-pointed in a way destructive to its original character. However, it must surely make a fine house in an even finer setting as soon as restoration is complete.

The buildings were quite crowded in the area of Wycoller House a hundred years ago for not only were there cottages across the road but there was a building in between. This building is only seen on the oldest photographs. Part of these premises was said to have been a shop during one period in its history.

Wycoller Cottage   Wycoller Cottage, alias Emmott's Cottage, formerly Wycoller Farm is an interesting old building. Thomas C. Emmott lived there

Cottage in front of Wycoller House once said to be a shop

from 1947 to 1964 and after his death it fell into ruin once again. In 1965 the Water Board sold the cottage to J. Plank of Preston for the sum of £300. The cottage has since changed hands and the owner has made excellent renovations. The floors have been damp-proofed and covered with parquet flooring, the original beams have been cleaned and stained and the interesting stonework has been left exposed, central heating has been installed and an ultra modern kitchen fitted.

On the ground at the end of Wycoller Hall stood a cottage for many years used as a chapel and school house. This is not to be confused with the later chapel which was in a cottage opposite Wycoller House on the other side of the water. A further cottage was attached to the end of the Hall of which nothing now remains. It did not extend the full width of the Hall end but traces of its shape can be seen in the wall. Other cottages were attached to the Hall and they were most likely separate dwellings throughout their history. A further cottage stood between the Hall and the barn.

Most of the books and articles that tell the story of Wycoller mention a Bobbin Mill which was supposed to have stood in the Dene. E. W. Folley describes the position in *Romantic Wycoller*:

Bobbin Mill

> *Proceed along the Dene, noting its wealth of bird and flowers, until the waterfall is reached. Here stood the bobbin-mill worked by the power of running water. David Haworth ran it . . . Since his father lived in a cottage behind the Hall there is some support for the idea that before a bobbin-mill stood over the fall, it was occupied by the estate's saw-mill. There is still a faint trace of the foundation of the building.*

There is no doubt that wood turning was carried on in Wycoller by David Haworth but no evidence has yet shown that any building ever stood in the place described. The building surely would have been shown on the detailed Tithe Map of 1844 and on the early Ordnance Survey map of 1848—but there is no trace on either. However, a bobbin-shop is shown on the Tithe Map but it was situated near the site of the present Thistleholme Cottage. David Haworth, the wood turner, came from Midgely near Halifax. He married a local girl and brought up a family of nine or ten children in Wycoller.

Before we leave our look at Wycoller's cottages we must consider one further point. When these cottages have been modernised with wall-to-wall carpets and central heating people will comment on how delightful it is to live in a seventeenth or eighteenth century cottage. It must be remembered that in their day these cottages were frequently cold, damp, ill furnished and dark. Their owners lived a hard life, often a short one, dying of typhoid, cholera and smallpox. The cottages had unhygienic toilet tubs which were emptied on the land, and the water they drank was frequently polluted by deadly germs. Modernisation and a romantic imagination may easily lead to a false appreciation of the past.

Field names

Field names are frequently recorded in old deeds but the most comprehensive source is the Tithe Award for Trawden made in 1844. Following the Tithe Award Act all those areas of the country where tithes had not already been changed to money payments were surveyed so that this reform could be completed. The Trawden Tithe Award consists of a rather unwieldly map about three metres long and an accompanying schedule. On the map all the farms, cottages and fields are numbered and the schedule is the key, giving the owner and occupier of the land, together with the land use, acreage and apportioned rent charge.

Although the surface of the Tithe Map is peeling through age and the field shapes have occasionally changed during the last hundred years, the majority of the field names have been identified and listed with numbered references to the modern Ordnance Survey Map. The Tithe Awards are frequently used as a basis from which to explore land use over many centuries. In many areas field names have remained unchanged over the centuries and farm holdings have remained static—but not in Wycoller. We have seen how frequently some farm names have been changed and the field names were no exception. There are many field names recorded in deeds during the century before the Tithe Award which had disappeared by 1844. The Smithfield Meadow, Robinson Close, Kiln Field, the Clough, the Mossy Banks, the Myrey Field, the Hawthorn Bed and the New Ing are some examples of this.

Of the few land names mentioned in the sixteenth century court rolls there is no trace in the 1844 lists—the Hempelands, the Swynecroft and a close called the Westsyde de le Hey. The field termed Hempelands in 1548 probably shows that this area was used for the cultivation of hemp or a similar fibre producing plant suitable for making sacking and rope. Tudor inventories show the possession of many sacks and lengths of sacking material. Roger Hartley had linen cloth, and flax may also have been grown locally at that time. As well as a change in field names land use has also changed and by 1844 there was not a great deal of arable land in Wycoller. However, there is evidence from plough marks that more of the valley had been under the plough during earlier centuries. As better communications developed it was easier for Wycoller to buy its wheat, oats and barley than to grow them.

Some fields have had their names varied by passing from mouth to mouth and document to document. Hellmishead Meadow became Hellman Heads and later Elmer Lead. To discover the original meaning of such names is just about impossible. Luckily most field names are self explanatory, the remains of the delph can be seen in Delf Field and the dried up fish pond in Fish Pond Field.

Following the General Enclosure Act of 1817 the common lands of Trawden Forest were shared between the copyholders of Trawden, Winewall and Wycoller in 1821. Each copyholder was given a portion of the commons in relationship to the amount of land he already owned. A plan of the allotments of Trawden Forest gives the impression that the individual plots were fenced with stone walls. This walling should have been carried out but the majority of land has remained unfenced to this day, especially on the slopes of Boulsworth where it is fit only for sheep. Not only did the copyholders not enclose the land but also they neglected to pay the rent to the lord of the manor. A letter from the Steward, Dixon Robinson, at Clitheroe Castle dated 31 March 1857 states, "I have received instructions to take more energetic measures for the purpose of enforcing the payment of the Rents payable to the Duke of Buccleuch under the Trawden Inclosures Act, and the award made in persuance of it. The rents are now several years in arrears, and it is quite impossible that the present system can be allowed to go on any longer". The landowners and farmers refused to pay any arrears but a compromise was reached after several meetings.

Trawden Enclosure Award 1821

We have looked at the farms and cottages and the fields that surround them and noted the constant change over the centuries. Buildings have served many purposes in their lifetimes and fields have been arable, pasture and meadow in the changing use of land. We should beware of coming to many conclusions from the evidence of an historic snapshot such as the 1844 Tithe Award.

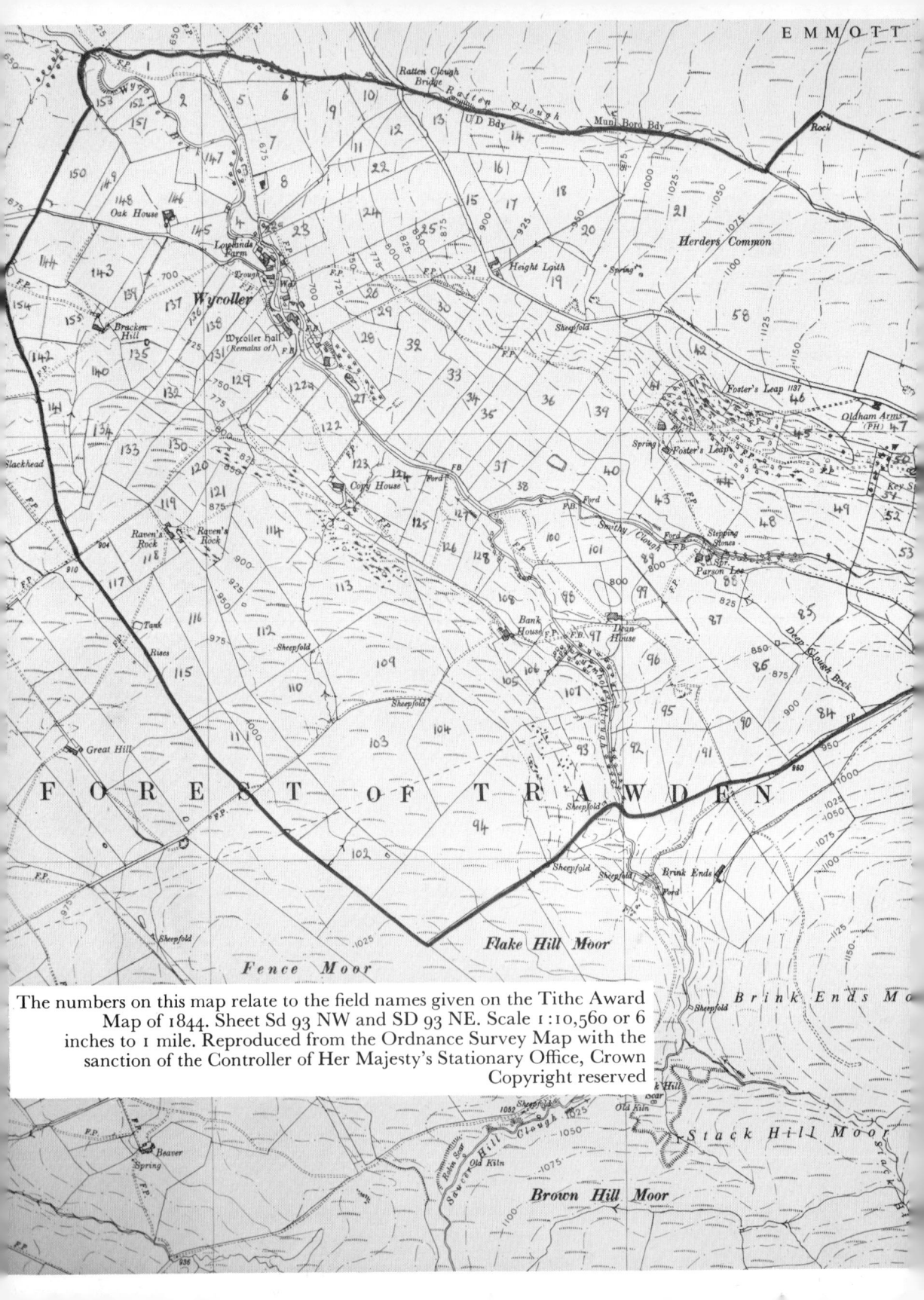

The numbers on this map relate to the field names given on the Tithe Award Map of 1844. Sheet Sd 93 NW and SD 93 NE. Scale 1:10,560 or 6 inches to 1 mile. Reproduced from the Ordnance Survey Map with the sanction of the Controller of Her Majesty's Stationary Office, Crown Copyright reserved

MOOR

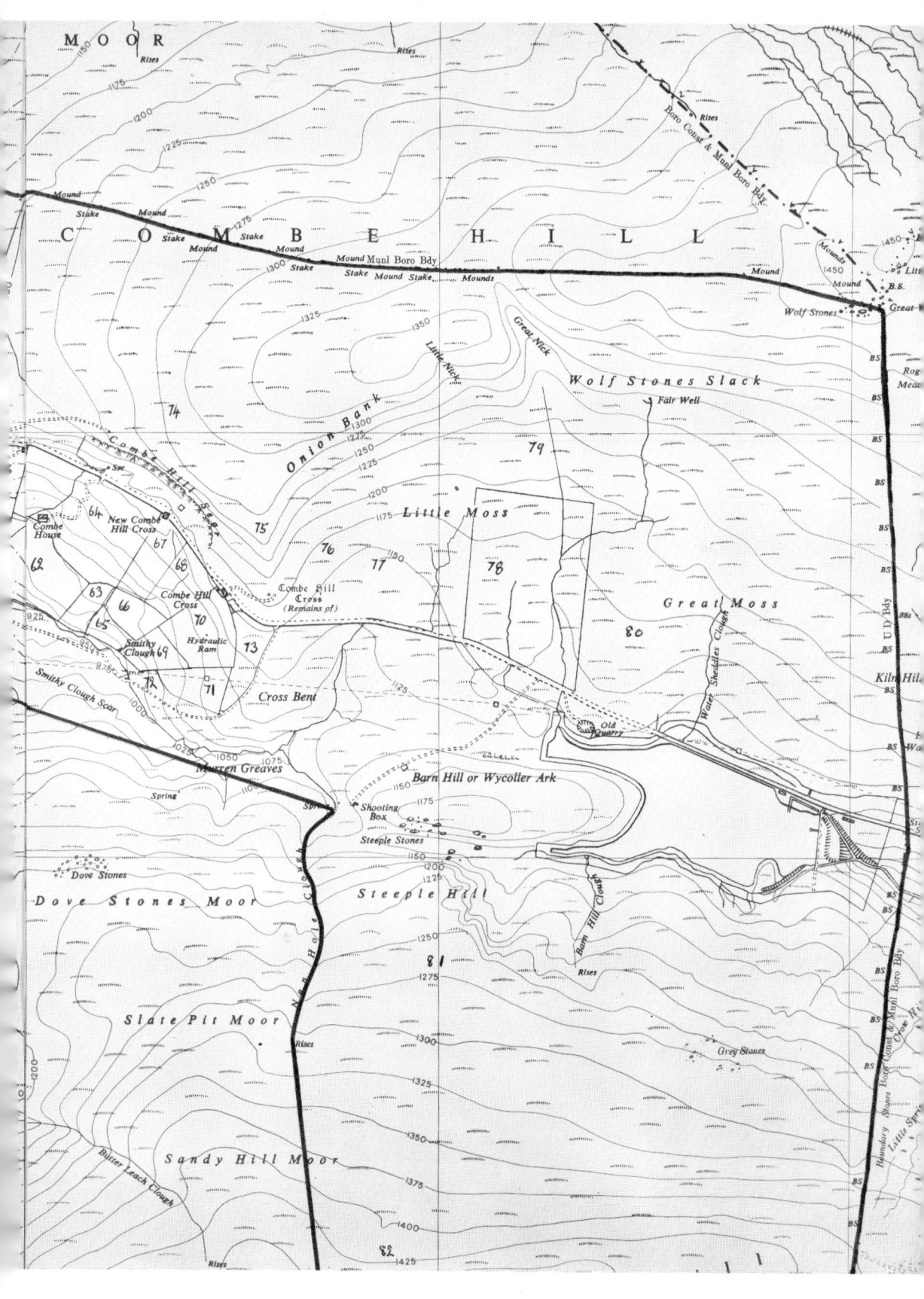

COMBE HILL

Wolf Stones Slack
Great Nick
Little Nick
Fair Well
Onion Bank
Little Moss
Great Moss
Wolf Stones
Water Sheddles Clough
Kiln Hill
Combe House
New Combe Hill Cross
Combe Hill Cross
Combe Hill Cross (Remains of)
Hydraulic Ram
Smithy Clough
Smithy Clough Scar
Cross Bent
Old Quarry
Murren Greaves
Spring
Barn Hill or Wycoller Ark
Shooting Box
Steeple Stones
Dove Stones
Dove Stones Moor
Steeple Hill
Barn Hill Clough
Slate Pit Moor
Grey Stones
Butter Leach Clough
Sandy Hill Moor

Wycoller Field Names from the Trawden Tithe Map of 1844

1. Thistle Holme
2. Thistle Meadow
3. Holme
4. Hare House Holme
5. Little Field
6. Low Field
7. Meadow
8. Great Meadow
9. Rough Bank
10. Coppy
11. Three Halfpenny Cake
12. Coppy
13. Little Long Field
14. Long Field
15. House Field
16. Little Field
17. Little Field
18. Middle Field
19. New Meadow
20. Old Meadow
21. Height Laithe Rough
22. Pepper Ing Field
22a Milking Hill
23. Lower Pepper Ing Field
24. Pepper Ing Field
25. Long Field
26. Tenter Field
27. Garden and Fishponds
28. Hall green and Potato bed
29. Wood
30. Hawthorn Field
31. Pike Hill
32. Hall Meadow
33. Great Foster Leap
34. Foster Leap
35. Foster Leap
36. Foster Leap
37. Bullions
38. Fish Pond Meadow
39. Horse Field Close
40. Height Field
41. Long Field
42. Crag Nook Field
43. Great Meadow
44. Crag Pasture
45. Well Plantation
46. Coppy
47. Herders Meadow
48. Little Wheatley
49. Great Wheatley
50. Croft
51. Uphill
52. Little Field
53. Coppy
54. Meadow
55. Uphill
56. Road Hill
57. Turf Meadow
58. Herders
59. Common
60. Herders Field
61. Common
62. Great Meadow
63. Scar Field
64. Broad Field
65. Cote Bank
66. Cote Meadow
67. Near Croft Field
68. Near Croft Meadow
69. Low Field
70. Cross Meadow
71. Cross Field
72. Common
73. Common
74. Common
75. Common
76. Common
77. Common

164

78. Common
79. Common
80. Common
81. Common
82. Common
83. Out Laithe Meadow
84. Great Marl
85. Thistle Lands
86. Round Hill
87. Higher Meadow
88. Potato Bed
89. Long Field
90. Black Hill Hole
91. Black Hill Hole
92. Turn Hole Cote
93. Stone
94. Great Rough
95. Delf Field
96. Higher Meadow
97. Fothering Holme
98. Higher Cow Hey
99. Lower Meadow
100. Lower Cow Hey
    Stirpenden 1803
101. New Meadow
102. New Piece
103. Moss
104. Little Rough
105. Bank
106. Little Field
107. Great Field
108. Great Meadow
109. New Ground
110. Wallet
111. Rough
112. Rush Bed
113. Crank
114. Middle Field
115. Great Field
116. Ashes Field
117. Laithe Field
118. New Meadow
119. Croft
120. Dripping Stone Field
121. Delf Field
122. Near Meadow
122a Further Meadow
123. Meadow
124. Coppy
125. Coppy
126. New Meadow
127. Little Meadow
128. Middle Meadow
129. Muck Dole
130. Elmer Lead
    Hellman Heads 1823
    Hellmishead Meadow 1750
131. Laithe Hill
132. Laithe Hill
133. Great Meadow
134. Elmer Lead
135. Delf Field
136. Long Meadow
137. Bracken Hill Meadow
138. Laithe Hill
139. Kirk Hill Dyke
140. House Field
141. Highmost Field
142. Mole Field
143. Rough Field
144. Higher Bent
145. Balwin Croft
    Baldwin's Croft 1818
146. Laithe Field
147. Great Meadow
148. Three Nooked Field
149. Lower Bent
150. Lower Bent
151. Little Meadow
152. Stoney Bent Holme
153. Thistle Holme
154. Fish Pond Field
155. Laithe End Close

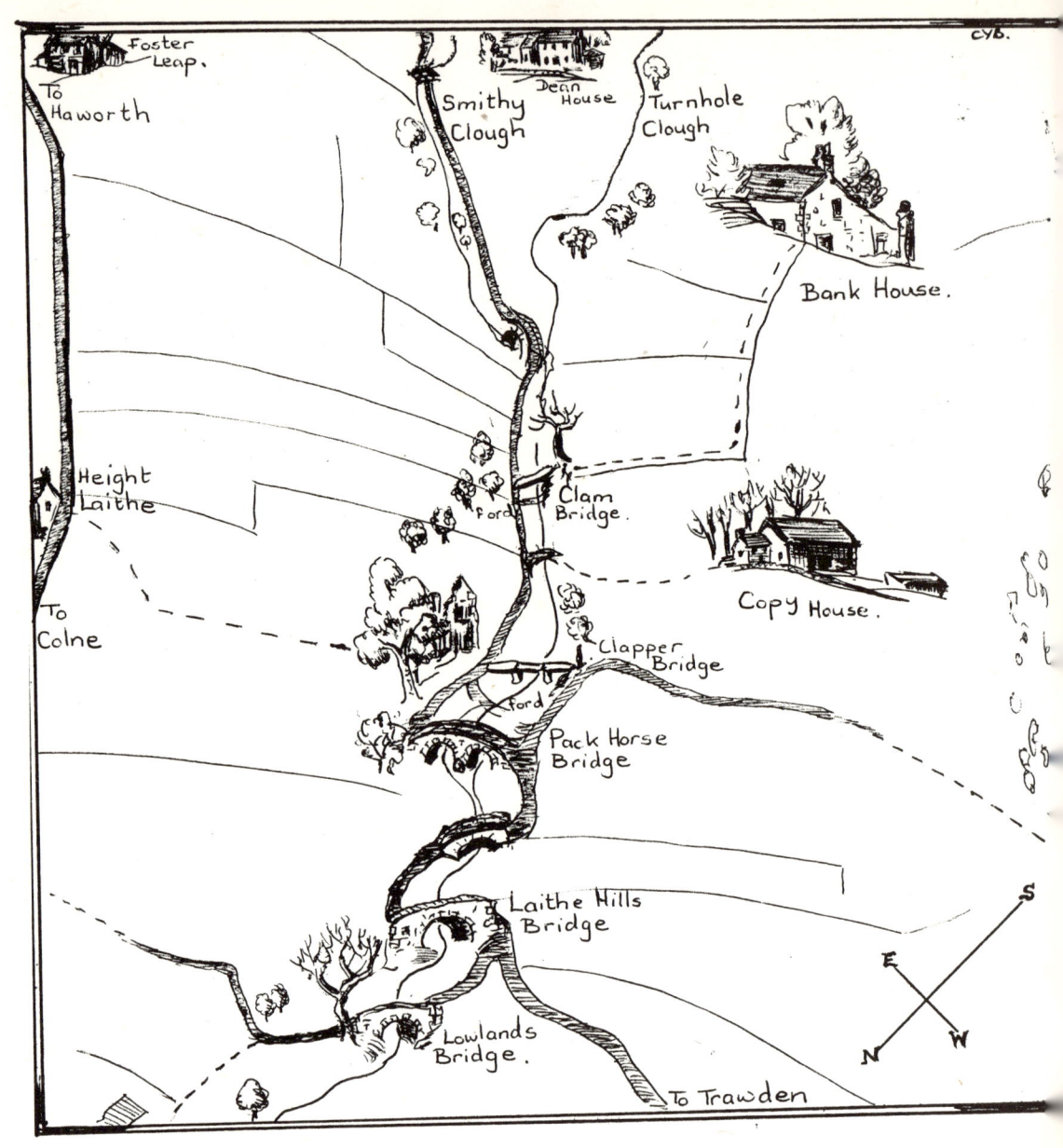

Artistic plan of Wycoller's bridges

166

Valley of the Seven Bridges

It is impossible to write a history of bridges in England without taking note of the Wycoller valley. Here within the space of the village and a quarter of a mile of the Dene beyond it are seven or eight bridges, several fords and the remains of stepping stones. There is no doubt that this should be considered one of Wycoller's main claims to fame and a strong case for the preservation of the bridges as they now exist. From where the lane enters Wycoller village at Lowlands Farm to the water meetings in the Dene there are eight bridges but, the title *Valley of the Seven Bridges* has been retained because of its traditional use.

Our close look at the bridges of Wycoller begins where the lane from Laneshawbridge nears Lowlands Farm. Lowlands Bridge takes us across the stream and into the farm yard. Before we cross we should note the old ford which lies not many metres down stream of the bridge. Lowlands Bridge seems little altered since it was originally built as the stones under the arch are matching and regular. There is a tradition that the bridge was constructed from the arch of the cellars of Wycoller Hall. The stones, it is said, were

Lowlands Bridge

Lowlands Bridge

167

Old Lowlands water supply

marked one by one and then re-erected to form the bridge. A slightly varying version of the story says that the stones came from the old ice house at the Hall.

Laithe Hills Bridge

The road now runs along the right bank of the stream and shortly joins the road from Trawden at Laithe Hills. Here the road crosses the stream passing back to the left bank over Laithe Hills Bridge. This bridge has been considerably widened over the last years. The underside of the arch has been extended twice in its lifetime on the last occasion with reinforced concrete. Very likely the first bridge at this site was an old pack-horse bridge; a ford for carts passes up stream of the bridge.

We cross the third bridge in the valley as we approach Pearson's Farm. This bridge brings us back to the right bank. The bridge has much in common with Lowlands Bridge and leads past Pearson's

Laithe
Hills
Bridge

Farm and Wycoller House to the widest part of the valley floor with buildings on both banks. Here the road leads to the ford across the stream, a ford which has existed since four wheeled traffic first ran in the valley and it is still the only crossing place for vehicles to gain access to the road up the Dene.

Alongside the ford are the remains of stepping stones, a few yards to the left of the ford is a fine old pack-horse bridge and a few yards to the right a rare clapper bridge. Why so many methods of crossing the stream came to be made within such a few metres is a question that has been asked many times and will probably never be answered to everyone's satisfaction. Why was it not possible for pack-horses to use the ford? Why could cattle and pack-horses not use the clapper bridge? How old are these fascinating historic bridges?

Possibilities are all that can be suggested. Perhaps when the stream was in flood the burden of a heavily laden pack-horse might touch the water and make a bridge essential. Perhaps the older clapper bridge was unsuitable for cattle and pack-horses because of a hand-rail for people on foot. Perhaps in earlier days a wall ran down to the stream and access to the clapper bridge was not readily available. One thing is certain it is due to the width and shallowness of the stream, the close proximity of the buildings and

Voussoirs or arch stones under the pack-horse bridge

the relative poverty of the village that a road bridge was not constructed here. Had it been, then it is unlikely that the other historic bridges would have survived intact.

Pack-horse bridge

The pack-horse bridge is a two arched bridge of fascinating construction. It is frequently said to be a thirteenth century erection but some attribute it to be fifteenth century. It may well be much later than this and we will never know its true age although it has stood there for centuries and withstood the constant traffic of man and pack-horse trains. The bridge construction is of interest for several reasons. The voussoirs, or arch shaped stones, extend the complete width of the bridge and for a considerable time the arch stones themselves were the actual paving of the bridge and showed considerable wear. Also the base stone boulders themselves not being level, the bridge is given a precarious appearance. The Ministry of Works reported on the bridge in 1948.

Ministry of Works report

At first glance this appears to be in a precarious state but it is considered mainly an optical effect due to the extraordinary method employed in springing the arch (entirely of long stones) direct from the rock without any attempt to level it first; the distortion of the arch does not appear to be a recent fault and in fact may never have been true. The bridge is not falling over as appearances suggest. Mortar in the joints is mainly lacking and they should be thoroughly consolidated.

> *The original path surface and low parapets are missing and the backs of the arch stones now form the surface. When this is washed out and consolidated, it would perhaps be as well to lay a layer of concrete over the whole bridge, within the parapets of course, to form a saddle and provide a proper surface, care, however, would be necessary to provide a pleasing surface.*
>
> *The bridge is now mainly used by cattle and an opinion was sought whether these were likely to cause the collapse of the bridge. It is not considered that they will do any immediate damage though there is no apparent reason why they should not use the ford except in time of exceptional flood.*

The pack-horse bridge is frequently referred to as Sally's Bridge. Tradition has it that a lady of that name was responsible for it being built. It is interesting to speculate that the Sally in question was not the builder, such a story being hardly credible, but Squire Henry Cunliffe's niece, Sally Scargill, who delighted in her stays at Wycoller both as a child and later in life. Sarah Scargill, or Sally as she was generally known, later became Sally Owen and mother of the last squire Henry Owen Cunliffe.

People often remark how marvellous it is that the bridge has been able to withstand the passage of time and yet remain so complete. Although basically true, the bridge has come near to destruction several times. Early pictures show loose arch stones in the first arch crossing from the village towards the Hall. When Major General C. H. Owen visited Wycoller in 1884 he wrote that the bridge was in a very dilapidated state and that the keystone of one of the arches had dropped. The top walling too has disappeared from time to time often being replaced in a different style.

Clapper bridge

Crossing the stream by the Hall is the clapper bridge, a large primitive bridge of massive proportions. Clapper bridges of this quality are rare and there is considerable disagreement about their age. The clapper bridge at Wycoller ranks along with that at Postbridge in Devon as one of the most interesting early bridges in England. Whether they are two thousand years old or less than a thousand, their construction is of the most primitive kind. In *Romantic Wycoller* and in some other accounts of Wycoller you will read that the clapper bridge consists of two great slabs of stone, the inner ends of which rest on a central pier. If you visit Wycoller to take a look yourself you will see that the clapper bridge has three large slabs of gritstone and rests on two piers.

Clapper bridge and pack-horse bridge

However, the bridge was probably originally constructed with two long blocks supported on a central pier. At some time in the last century it is said that the slab on the Hall side was split by the fall of a heavy tree. In early photographs taken before 1900 this side of the bridge is seen to be supported by a log of oak. That support has been replaced with a firm pier and other repair work has been carried out. Centuries of use wore a deep trough in the centre of the slabs. Unfortunately, this record of the wear of the clogs of many generations of weavers was destroyed around the year 1910. The Rev. C. S. Sargisson wrote in 1911, "Now, alas!

172

Deep trough worn in clapper bridge

the stone is smooth enough, and an invaluable record has been sacrificed to the convenience of any local magnate who may occasionally pass that way, or to that of the trippers who visit this beauty-spot in thousands during the summer".

The clapper bridge is also the Hall Bridge, the Weavers' Bridge and the Druids' Bridge. Its varying names reflect both its great age and the traditions that surround it. It is the Hall Bridge because it leads to the Hall. It is the Weavers' Bridge because in times gone by it was used by generations of handloom weavers who lived in the village. It is the Druids' Bridge because legend has it that it led to an amphitheatre where the druids held human sacrifices.

Crossing to the Hall side of the stream the road continues up the Dene on the left bank and very soon a bridge spans the stream leading to Copy House on the right. Further along a solid slab of gritstone spans the stream appearing at first, because of its great length, to be a huge tree trunk. Although apparently precariously perched on the road bank the slab is quite firm and has stood the test of time. This clam bridge is the most primitive form of bridge only one step beyond the simple tree trunk. At one time the bridge had a rail at one side for the safety of those who crossed and the small post holes can still be seen in the stone. A ford once crossed the beck immediately down stream of the bridge and many large vaccary stones remain embedded in the stream bed.

Clam bridge

Clam bridge

The last bridge that we have to take account of is found at the water meetings where Parson Lee Clough and Turn Hole Clough join together. The original bridge has gone and the present bridge is of modern construction and little interest. The original bridge on this site was often referred to, without any justification, as the Roman Bridge. The bridge was a simple arch of single stone thickness yet the blocks, or rather rough pieces of stone, were put together so cleverly that for years they withstood the passage of heavy farm carts.

In 1966 a ninth bridge made of timber was erected on stone foundations within touching distance of the pack-horse bridge. The builder, J. Holdsworth of Parson Lee Farm, was ordered to demolish the bridge as it had been built without planning permission. The

Wycoller Dene

The old bridge that once stood by the water meetings

stone foundations can still be seen on the Hall bank of the stream. The Water Board was sympathetic even when ordering this construction to be removed. In spite of all the bridges, we have seen that the only way to the Dene for vehicles is through the ford, which during floods causes much difficulty for cars. Unfortunately any sort of bridge at this point would spoil the character of Wycoller.

Had Wycoller existed anywhere but in its remote moorland valley surely by now a motor road would have caused the loss of the bridges, the loss of cottages and the loss of much of the beauty of the Dene and village. Luckily preserved by its remoteness, this valley, with its wandering stream, has left to posterity a fascinating collection of historic bridges.

Saved from the Flood

The growing Victorian town of Colne was in need of water and when the Colne Corporation looked around for a convenient site to construct a reservoir Wycoller appeared a natural choice. They found the remote, steep sided Wycoller valley ideal; there a dam could be built across the south eastern end of the valley, and the waters of the Wycoller Beck would do the rest. The main landowner in the valley was Susanah Benson, daughter of Richard Hartley, and the Corporation began the process of negotiation in 1896. Susanah Benson was far from pleased for she loved the village of Wycoller and the beautiful dene beyond it. The village was always kept spick and span in her days and she took great delight in its orderliness.

Reservoir scheme

Disconcerted though she was over the proposed flooding of the valley, Susanah Benson was also unhappy about the manner in which the Colne Corporation proposed to organise the compulsory purchase of her land. The Corporation wished to buy only slightly more land than the area of the actual reservoir they planned to construct. They wished to take half a field here and half a meadow there and of course the land they wanted being the lowest in the valley was also the best. In all they wished to take about fifty acres of the best meadow and pasture from the various farms on her land the result of which Susanah Benson saw would be chaos. The farm buildings would be rendered useless, and the farms and fields would be so severed that the portions left would be of little use. In view of this she decided to lodge a petition against the waterworks section of the bill.

The bill that Colne put to Parliament was, "a Bill for making further and better provision in regard to the Water Supply, and the improvement, Health, and Good Government of the Borough of Colne, and for other purposes". This bill provided for the construction of North Valley Road, a refuse destructor, a technical institution, extension to the burial ground and the construction of a waterworks. The reservoir at Wycoller was to be a compensatory reservoir. The Corporation had two gathering grounds in mind but at first it was proposed to take only one of them with a capacity of one hundred and twenty million gallons. If and when the population of Colne grew further then the second gathering ground could be utilised.

    The surprising fact about the proposed reservoir at Wycoller is that it would not have flooded one building, An embankment three hundred and fourteen metres long was to be built across the valley about two hundred metres up the dene from Wycoller Hall. On the east side of Wycoller Beck the water would rise only a third of the way up the fields to Height Laithe Farm, while on the west side the water would extend to within a few metres of Copy House and about one hundred metres from Bank House. Both Parson Lee and Dean House would lie well clear of the water line at the top end of the reservoir. At the deepest point the reservoir would be twenty metres deep. The fact that no buildings would be submerged did not infer that Wycoller could have survived the flood with little damage. New roads would have had to be cut through the valley and aqueducts would have traced their conspicuous courses in many directions, at one point cutting through the Hall grounds. Wycoller

Artists impression of Wycoller Dene had the Wycoller reservoir been constructed

Hall and the unoccupied cottages would have been used as a quarry for readily accessible stone and rubble. As the Old Hall Cottage was used to build a chlorinator plant at Bents reservoir and provide rubble for the waterworks road there, so too the cottages of Wycoller would likely have disappeared in waterworks construction.

A public meeting held at Colne Town Hall on 8 January 1897 had to be adjourned to the Cloth Hall because of the large attendance. Although there was no dissention recorded at the meeting, opposition grew later and, in February, Trawden protested that the new Waterworks would affect their own water rights and possibly affect their rates. Nowhere was there any word of protest against the flooding of a wooded dene as delightful as any in the country. Trawden's farmers were concerned over the loss of water and insisted that Trawden should have "everything belonging to it". However, when it came to active opposition the fact that it might prove expensive dampened their ardour and the opposition melted away.

Public meeting

When the final list of petitions against the bill was filed there were few. Carr and Sons solicitors of Colne were angry because many petitions prepared by them had not been filed. In a letter to the *Colne Times* of 26 February 1897 they stated that they had prepared

Plan of the reservoir

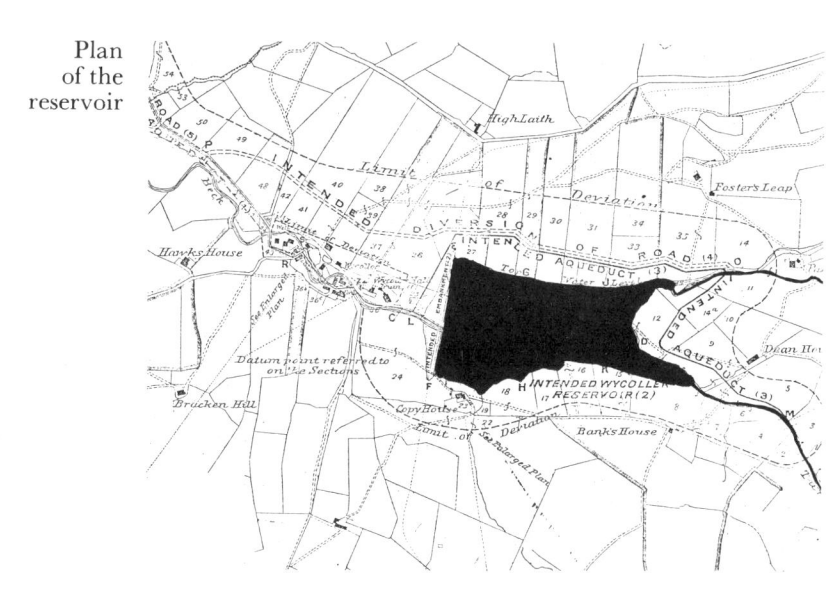

a petition for "Mrs. Susanah Benson of Wycoller, against the waterworks provision of the bill". They complained that the petitioners had been intimidated by Colne Borough Council who had informed them that they would have to pay full costs of the opposition.

Susanah Benson dropped her petition because she had come to terms with the Colne Corporation. Matthew Watson of Burnley, surveyor and valuer, had been retained by Carr and Sons to advise on the Wycoller question. He was efficient and forceful, and as a result of his proposals Colne Corporation agreed to buy the complete farms. They bought Bank House farm, Wycoller Hall farm, Pearson's farm and Hawks House farm from Susanah Benson, and she dropped her petition only when this was agreed on. The Borough Surveyor of Colne, F. H. Hartley, signed the agreement on the area of the Benson property on 1 March 1897 and financial agreement soon followed. The Corporation acquired the farms and 162 acres 1 rood and 2 perches of land for the sum of £9,898. At the same time they bought Dean House and Copy House farms from J. W. C. Ayre and Mrs. Smith.

The bill passed through Parliament and work began on the many schemes. However, the costs of the Wycoller reservoir project were going to be heavy. Over £10,000 had already been paid for the land and it had been estimated that over £100,000 would be needed to complete the work. The project was delayed. The Corporation were made aware that there was a possible alternative; if underground water could be discovered then the reservoir project could be cancelled or at least shelved for a few years.

Wycoller Bore Hole Professor Boyd-Dawkins, an eminent geologist of the day, was retained to survey the Wycoller area. He was convinced that water could be found if bore holes were sunk among the rocks at Wycoller and he indicated four places which he considered the most promising. The Corporation consented to a trial and Matthews of Manchester were employed as contractors. Serious work on boring began in the summer of 1901 and from the start the work suffered one set back after another, mainly due to the failure of the steam engine which powered the drills. The Mayor, Alderman Robinson Foulds, had a disappointing story to report to the Corporation on several occasions, and many began to consider the project a waste of time and money.

The breakthrough came in September when water was discovered at four hundred and twenty feet and pumping operations began. "Water Discovered At Last" the press announced and everyone including the Corporation were greatly relieved. Water was a pressing problem in 1901 and the issue of the *Colne and Nelson Times*, of 4 October 1901, which reported the bore hole's progress also reported water riots in the adjoining town of Nelson. Officials of the Water Committee drove out to Wycoller by waggonette on Thursday 6 September and inspected the site. Dr Lovett took a sample of the water and found it to be soft and in his opinion admirable drinking water. The water, however, was not to be used for consumption but purely to supply the stream at Wycoller so that equivalent water could be taken from Laneshawbridge and Bonny Booth for Colne's domestic supply.

A. Wilmore, F.G.S., of Colne, discussed the geological aspects of the water discovery at Wycoller in the local press. He explained that we live in what the geologist calls a huge basin, stretching from Pendle to Boulsworth. He further explained that there were basins within basins and that one such basin stretched from the uplands above Laneshawbridge on the north side to Watersheddles hills on the other side. The rocks at Knarrs, at Shayhead and at Alma dip towards Wycoller. The rocks at Brink Ends, Emmott Moor and Combe Hill also dip towards Wycoller. Dr. Wilmore felt that it was highly likely that the rocks that stand out on the highlands on either side pass right down under Wycoller and under the little coalfield in the lower part of the Wycoller valley. If these were the rocks which the bore hole had tapped then they derived their water from a massive area of moorland above Wycoller on the south and a considerable area on the north side. The rain falling on these gathering

Local geology

Inaugeration ceremony at Wycoller bore hole

grounds, he said, sank through the earth and porous rock to find its way underground into the natural trough of water-bearing rock. The amount of rain the area receives was an important factor but with an average rainfall of over forty inches a year he believed that there should be no shortage of underground water in the Wycoller area.

In the 1930s when water became short again the question of the Wycoller reservoir was revived. Although no work had ever been carried out, the Colne Corporation still retained powers for the waterworks. On this occasion Councillor E. A. Foulds, Chairman of the Water Committee, was responsible for persuading the council to seek the advice of a geological expert on the possibility of obtaining additional water supply from underground sources. The Corporation knew that the only alternative was "the construction of the Wycoller reservoir, for which Parliamentary powers were first obtained in 1897, but on which the Town Council had always been reluctant to embark because of its magnitude and costliness". No mention was made that it would save Wycoller Dene from flooding, only that the Corportion was reluctant to build the reservoir because of its "magnitude and costliness". Once again underground water was discovered and on 10 June 1938 the Corn Close bore hole just off the Colne to Cowling road was officially inaugurated— Wycoller had gained a second reprieve.

The site of the Wycoller bore hole covers about half an acre yet the Water Committee found themselves the reluctant landlords of six farms, two cottages and two hundred and fifty six acres of land. From the evidence of their records the main aim of the Water Department was to spend as little as possible on the village of Wycoller. The reports were always keen to stress that the minimum had been spent. In 1928 the Water Engineer's report stated, "The cost of repairs was lower than in the previous year, the amount being £80 odd as against £137". These figures included all the Water Department's property including Wycoller. In 1929 £60 was spent on repairs and the Water Engineer was pleased to report that this was "Very small".

It must be recorded that in 1928 the Water Department did show some concern about the ruins of Wycoller Hall. In February of that year they pulled down "some dangerous walls of Wycoller Hall" and considered the preservation of the ruins. They reported that "The part belonging to the Corporation had been straightened up and made safe, and the owner of the remaining portion had been approached and asked to consider transferring it to the custody of the Corporation on the undertaking to keep it in proper condition as an old structure of historical interest". The owner, Watson Benson, replied that he would let the Corporation have it for £1,000.

The Water Engineer seemed ill-fated to deal with tenants and repairs. In November 1928 he was put to the test when he admitted William Bracewell as a tenant farmer. In 1934 William Bracewell wanted a shippon at Laithe Hills Farm to house eighteen cattle rather than the eight he could house at the time. In 1936 the barn roof at Wycoller Farm had collapsed and had to be stripped and reconstructed at a cost of £100. The roof at Laithe Hills Farm was little better and the Water Engineer noted in his report of 8 July 1936 that the main barn roof was in poor condition. In his 1937 report the Water Engineer reported that the roof had given way through decay and, "That renewal would have necessitated considerable repair and you therefore decided to have the place pulled down and entirely rebuilt". William Bracewell had pulled it off, influencing the Water Engineer who in his turn had influenced the Water Committee, and his new cowshed and dairy was built.

The Water Engineer then had to inform William Bracewell that his rent had been raised by £25 per annum and he was surprised when the farmer not only refused to pay, but also turned down a compromise offer of £15. He wrote in his report, "It appears to be a difficult matter to make an increase in rent unless the tenant consents to pay the same". Agreement was eventually reached and William Bracewell agreed to pay the £15 increase, but as crafty as as ever he agreed only on the undertaking that the Water Department would put a new bath and hot water in the farmhouse.

Collapsing roofs

Roof collapses occurred with monotonous regularity in Wycoller and they were not a sign of either good tenants or efficient landlords. In 1934 a large part of the roof at the Old Hall Cottage collapsed and had to be repaired. In 1936 the barn roof at Wycoller farm collapsed and in 1937 the roof of the barn at Laithe Hills did the same. In the same year of 1937 another cottage roof gave way. In 1946 the roof of Pepper Hill barn fell in and the same year the roof of the Old Hall Cottage collapsed once again. Excuses can be found as these were the lean years of the thirties and the austere years of the war but there must have been few running repairs or regular inspections of property by either landlords or tenants. The village of Wycoller was going to ruin.

Friends and Preservation

In July 1946, owing to extreme neglect, part of the roof of the Old Hall Cottage collapsed. The Colne Water Department noted in their annual report that "as the premises were in other ways becoming very dilapidated, it was decided to terminate the tenancy of the Colne Lads' Club and pull down the building. A considerable amount of the stone has been removed for use in building the proposed chlorinator plant at Bents reservoir and for its approach road".

This cottage was part of Wycoller Hall. Some seventy or eighty years ago the north-east wing, which included the old kitchen of the hall, was repaired and converted into a cottage. It was this wing of the Hall that the inhabitants of Wycoller and visitors to the village saw being demolished and removed waggon load, after waggon load to make a waterworks approach road. The Water Department claimed that they were not touching the Hall, but if they believed this then their ignorance is difficult to understand for the knowledge had been included in local books for fifty years. The ignorance and narrow-sightedness of the Water Department did not end there, for having demolished the Hall Cottage, the water engineer, F. R. Boothman, requested permission to demolish the remains of Wycoller Hall itself. The reason given was that children

Old Hall Cottage

playing in the ruins might suffer injury. Perhaps this was a reasonable fear but demolition was not the only answer.

It was inevitable that someone sooner or later would take up arms on behalf of Wycoller Hall. Many were depressed as they saw the ruins deteriorating year by year until, nettle-grown and collapsing, they were in danger of becoming an eyesore rather than a charm. Many more were now appalled at the wanton destruction of the village. Evelyn Jowett, the librarian at Colne, began canvassing friends in the area but she knew well that she would have to arouse the interest of some established body or, failing that, a new body would have to be formed.

Evelyn Jowett contacted the Brontë Society as Wycoller claimed strong Brontë connections and as many of those interested in Wycoller were also members of the Brontë Society. However, the Brontë Society were not keen to extend their interests so far from Haworth on the tenuous claim that Wycoller Hall was the Ferndean Manor of *Jane Eyre*. The society did show interest and willingness to give a grant should a local preservation group be formed. Miss Jowett now knew that she would have to get things organised locally.

Evelyn Jowett

A meeting of representatives of local organisations was held in the council chamber at Colne Town Hall on 3 July 1948. The second world war was over and the austerity that followed it had slackened enough to allow thought to be turned to things of culture and the thoughts of preserving them for the future. The Mayor of Colne, Alderman J. W. Shackleton was in the chair that evening, and there were representatives from Colne Corporation, Colne Camera Club, the Society for the Preservation of Ancient Buildings, the Brontë Society, Colne Literary and Scientific Society, Steeton Field Naturalist Society, Providence Rambling Club, Colne Public Library, Colne Dramatic Society, the Women's Social Services Club, the Co-operative Women's Guild (Colne) and the Cowling Women's Institute.

In welcoming everyone to the meeting the chairman explained that it had been necessary to begin some preliminary enquiries before the meeting as there were difficulties concerning the question of ownership of Wycoller Hall. The Town Clerk, L. A. Venables, explained that part of the Hall belonged to Colne Corporation and a further part to Herbert Richard Hartley of Rimington. For any thing effective to be done about the Hall, it would first have to be brought under unified ownership. Colne Corporation had no objection to works of preservation being carried out, provided that, as it was purchased as part of the Wycoller reservoir scheme, the property should be available for water purposes if ever the need should arise. When H. R. Hartley was approached he said that in his view the property was for the benefit of Colne ratepayers, "who go there at weekends for a little recreation," and he was not prepared to present it to Colne Corporation, although he would be willing to consider an offer for it.

The Colne Corporation made it quite clear that they had no intention of spending any money on restoration on behalf of Colne ratepayers. Their attitude was that the Hall was not in the Borough of Colne and interested parties would have to raise money necessary for preservation. The meeting came to the conclusion that an independent body should be set up to preserve not only the Hall, but also the surrounding area, including the two old bridges.

The important outcome of that first meeting was that the outlook

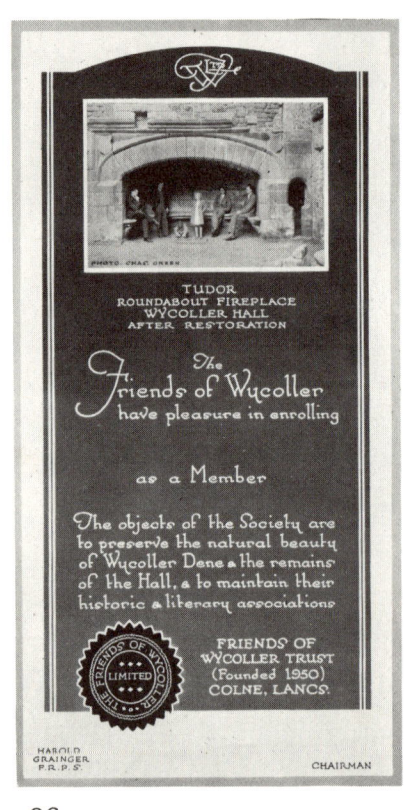

Membership card of the Friends of Wycoller

had been widened to consider not only the Hall but other parts of the village, and this was reflected in their chosen name—the Friends of Wycoller. The evening had also showed that there would be many difficulties. Firstly, though they had a great desire to preserve Wycoller Hall it was not theirs to preserve, and the owner of only half the ruin had asked for two thousand pounds. Secondly, were they to gain the Hall, a great deal of money would be needed for the preservation work.

Friends of Wycoller

Work and planning progressed rapidly in August and September 1948. Officials were elected and got to work. Within a few weeks E. W. Folley and Alderman G. E. Wilmore had been successful in persuading H. R. Hartley of Rimington to give them the eastern half of the Hall and the land immediately adjoining. This was great news, and shortly after Colne Corporation announced that they would transfer their interest in the Hall to the Friends.

In the early days the Friends of Wycoller were efficient, speedy and business-like. Without delay they affiliated with the Central Council of Civic Societies and the Society for the Preservation of Ancient Buildings. Even before a constitution was drawn up it was resolved "that the Town Clerk should write to the Ministry of Works and the Society for the Preservation of Ancient Buildings to ascertain the time required by them to prepare a report with the relative cost".

When the Ministry of Works report arrived it caused quite a shock. The two Ministry representatives had visited the village on 28 September and made a comprehensive examination of the Hall. They confirmed that the recently demolished cottage must have contained part at least of the original hall and made full recommendations for preservation. The sting was in the tail for the report estimated that the cost of preservation would be from five to six thousand pounds.

A less ambitious scheme had to be considered and it was decided to do the work in stages as funds became available. Time had first to be spent in recruiting members and raising money. The library committee gave permission for a collection box to be placed in the library and appeals were distributed as widely as possible. The pamphlets stressed the links between Wycoller and the Brontës, not the village's strongest claim to recognition, but one they knew would bring the maximum return.

Responses poured in from far and wide as the news spread. Lydia

Wyld of Hurstwood House, Hurstwood, sent one pound to Evelyn Jowett to set the ball rolling and Tom Emmott became the first subscriber after the appeal. Donations came in from all parts of the country, from Cornwall to Scotland. Members of the Cunliffe family were sprinkled amongst the subscribers, including Walter R. Cunliffe of Surrey and William L. Cunliffe of New York. Money was not only donated by the Brontë Society and many other local societies but also by many business concerns. Colne Operatic Society produced Frank Slater's *Wycoller* and gave the proceeds to the Friends, and celebrated personalities such as Dr. Phyllis Bentley and Robert Neil came to Colne to support the cause.

N. H. Hartley of Colne volunteered his architectural services and together with builder. L. Bond, he made an inspection of the ruins of Wycoller Hall in September 1949. They limited their attention to the southern portion of the ruins and in particular to the fire-place and the surrounding area. The mortar in the walls of the fire-place and flue was found to be perished and the masonry was being forced apart by tree roots with which the wall was filled. Rain had entered the wall and washed out loose mortar, and the upper courses of stones were in immediate danger of falling into the fire-place. The collapse of the rear and one side wall of the flue had already made the structure unstable. The fire-place arch was spreading due to the unequal loading and the loss of its lateral supports. At the same time the gable wall at the rear of the fire-place, the west wall and the mullioned windows were examined, reported on and recommendations made.

Flag laying at Wycoller Hall

Of course the work was not done at once, workers had to be recruited and organised, and tools and materials had to be bought or borrowed. Operations were begun in the corner of the fire-place where the key-hole niche is situated. Yard by yard dirt and rubble were removed to show the original floor level. The original flagstones had long been removed but the correct level was apparent by the sand upon which the original flagstones had been laid. New flagstones were offered by G. T. Spencer of Messrs George Rushworth & Son Ltd., six tons of them, and they were delivered free to Wycoller Hall. However, many tons of rubble had to be removed before the new flags could be laid.

1950 was a year of great activity at Wycoller Hall, trees endangering the foundations were removed, the floor was fully cleared and the fire-place restored. The restoration of the fire-place was a focal point of the operation. It took a considerable time and its completion was heralded by a blaze of publicity. A doorway, previously walled up, was opened to allow better access. In 1951 the passage behind the fire-place was cleared and the rubble and masonry were used to build a new retaining wall to the river where it was encroaching

The Hall fire-place under restoration

A threat to the foundations is removed

upon the roadway in front of the Hall. Other rubble was used to level off the village green and a dummy wall was erected to retain the new level. The ash tree which was undermining the wall of the the Hall towards the village was felled and other roots and vegetation removed from the walls of the ruins.

The Friends were not only keen to preserve the Hall but also to improve the amenities of the village so that it would be a more pleasant place for visitors. Toilets were constructed in a portion of Pearson's Farm, Lowlands Bridge was repaired, roads were repaired and drained and a large number of daffodil bulbs were planted. They had a hard struggle as the farming standards in and around the village were low, with broken gates, fallen walls and manure heaps on the roads.

A great deal of work was done by the volunteers who came regularly to Wycoller to perform their labour of love. Charles Green organised and reported on the work of the volunteers in the early days. Of all the volunteers the work of Jim Mellelieu is most frequently mentioned and following his premature death things came almost to a standstill. Soon to the casual visitor it was as though nothing had been done. The Ministry of Works had foreseen this danger when they suggested that a caretaker might be necessary, for from their wide experience of sites throughout the country they knew that without regular attention the ruins would soon become overgrown again.

As years went by the society began to run out of steam. Meetings were poorly attended and subscriptions were low. In 1959 the treasurer had to reply to a subscriber, "Yours has, in fact, been the only contribution in the past year, and I have not felt it right to accept it without your concurrence." In 1960 an attempt was made to raise funds, to reclaim old members and to recruit new ones. Funds were low and the Friends had compulsory commitments especially in the form of insurance taken out to cover the voluntary workers. The appeal from the chairman, E. W. Folley, had a sad note: "If in the recent years your annual subscription faltered we beg you to revive or even increase it . . . We ask you, not in vain, we hope, to renew or enlarge your generous help. Act at once. Send as much as you can afford, by post or personally, to any of the Friends known to you."

Lydia Wild, who had given the first donation, regularly sent her subscription year after year. She had hoped for full restoration at Wycoller but became increasingly aware that it would not come in her time. When she died in 1961 she left ten pounds to the Friends, but the money was too late to be of use except to pay insurance bills and the petty administration that still clung to the Friends of Wycoller Ltd. Due to the influence of L. A. Venables the Friends had become a limited company in the early days which had not been of any great advantage though it had been costly in time and money. In March 1963 the Friends held their last meeting and quietly dissolved.

Within a year the question of Wycoller was to rise again. In 1964 Trawden Urban District Council called a meeting of interested parties. They wished to settle the question of whether there was a need to preserve Wycoller, whether anything could be done and if so how should it be done. The meeting was held at the Council Offices on 24 June 1964. A map appended to the letter sent out by the Trawden Council showed the layout of various farms and cottages and gave comments about each. "Dene Cottage—excellent condition", "Farm building with filthy yard open to road", "Barn—holed roof, dilapidated", "Laithe Hills Cottage—dilapidated, demolition approved". It was the "demolition approved" that stung the heart of Wycoller lovers and led to the formation of the Wycoller Preservation Committee.

Councillor Douglas Barber was in the chair at that meeting in June, and the first meeting of the Preservation Committee was held

Wycoller Preservation Committee

at his house on 14 August 1964. At that meeting a full committee was elected, a report on the possibility of Wycoller property being leased or sold was drawn up, and future policy was discussed. Douglas Barber was elected chairman and Maureen Alyward, of Thistleholme Cottage, was elected secretary. From the start Douglas Barber and Maureen Aylward were to play the leading roles, combining the work of publicity officer and treasurer with their other duties.

The Committee was successful in gaining wide publicity. Its activities were recorded not only in the *Evening Telegraph* and the *Colne Times* but also in the *Manchester Guardian*, the *Yorkshire Post*, the *Daily Telegraph* and the *Daily Express*. The reports gave the facts on Wycoller and roused interest on a national scale. Letters of indignation at Wycoller's condition came from many parts of the country. N. D. Bond of Wemdon, Somerset wrote to the *Colne Times*, Sir,

> *It was while on holiday near Colne that I visited something that I have heard described as a "festering sore on the countryside." This was a quote from a short talk given on the B.B.C., Home Service on August 30th. Frankly I was appalled by what I saw. Have no Lancastrians any feeling as to works and industry of their early ancestors? The unfortunate part of the whole story is to my mind that it is in the wrong part of the country, as I feel that were it in the South or South Western Counties some enterprising person would have made it a show place . . . As one who has never been North and was quite impressed why has nothing been done about publicising this place? . . . I think you Northerners are too busy hurrying South at holidays. You miss the gems on your own doorstep."*

The Committee had direct and practical aims. They saw that to bring any real improvement to Wycoller, more life must be brought to the village in the form of permanent inhabitants. They also saw that amenities for visitors in the form of catering and car parks would have to be provided. These aims brought them into direct contact with the North Calder Water Board, which had by now taken over the Colne Corporation Water Department. The Water Board was interested in water and water alone, there was little if any interest in the cottages or conditions in the village let alone any interest in the history and culture of the place.

However, the Preservation Committee pressed the Water Board to sell cottages in Wycoller and was successful. Having persuaded the Board to sell cottages to the public the society were then faced with doubts as to whether interested people could be found to buy them. They prepared plans for both eventualities; if the cottages were sold they would give help to the owners and all would be well, on the other hand should the cottages remain unsold they considered negotiating with the Water Board to buy these themselves. The Committee considered two methods of raising money for the project, the first was the usual method of coffee mornings, jumble sales and subscriptions, while the second was to form a non-profit-making trust company and to ask for subscribers. Having once bought the properties the company could then restore them or lease them to interested people to restore the buildings themselves.

In November 1965 the Water Board informed the Preservation Committee that they had accepted the offer of D. J. Plank of Preston for the purchase of Wycoller Cottage and the offer of R. J. Wood of Bury for Laithe Hills Cottage and that the transactions were proceeding. Encouraged by this the Preservation Committee put forward many other proposals to the Water Board hoping for a sympathetic ear. They wanted to gain a foothold in Wycoller themselves to acquire a place for the storage of equipment and the sale of postcards. They also wanted to see the village cleaned up and to gain the Board's assistance in doing this. "We trust you will not regard these suggestions as presumptuous. We feel that the Board are probably conscious of their responsibility for this unique corner of Lancashire and we would welcome the opportunity of discussing the future of the hamlet with you at some time convenient to yourself".

From the Water Board there was either no response to letters or late replies, they may have felt some responsibility but they had little interest to do anything about it. After a delay of four months the water engineer C. D. Barnes replied to one letter as follows:- "I refer to your letter of the 20th May this year, but regret that I am not in a position to make further observations at the present time on the question of Wycoller which is still under consideration by the Board."

The Water Board had earlier withdrawn its support for the Preservation Committee when its representative, Councillor K. Tunnacliffe of Trawden, resigned. His comment on resigning was: "I think this board has done everything it can for this committee, and I cannot see why we should be represented on it any more."

During the same period it was reported that the Water Board had been removing stone from Wycoller Hall to carry out repair work on the banks of the Wycoller Beck.

In their attempt to clean up the village the Friends of Wycoller had had trouble with local farmers although through long persistence they did manage to get a few walls repaired, gates fixed and manure heaps removed from the road. The Preservation Society had the same difficulties due to poor farming methods and negligent landlords. The village was regularly in a disgraceful condition and the cottages and barns were used as tips for farm refuse. The Water Board, the landlords, did not seem to be able to prevent the accellerated decay. When the Preservation Committee wished to repair the wall surrounding Wycoller Hall they wrote for permission to the Water Board. "As such walling would not prejudice the Board's interests in any way, we will assume that, in the absence of any word to the contrary, we can go ahead as planned." The Board refused permission for the wall to be repaired.

Farming conditions were so bad in Wycoller that complaints were received by both the Water Board and the Ministry of Agriculture. In 1965 the Ministry received a complaint about milk production at Oak House, "I have in mind a farm where cattle are milked in what appears to me to be deplorably unhygienic conditions The farm is filthy, the milking operative likewise, and the yard outside is often deep in mud. Milking is done by hand—there being no electricity—and the only available water is from a stream that flows alongside the nearby road."

The Friends of Wycoller and the Wycoller Preservation Committee played an important part in the story of Wycoller. There is no doubt that but for the work done by the Friends the Hall fireplace, a focal point for visitors, would have collapsed into a heap of rubble. The Preservation Committee too had their success in getting the Water Board to sell cottages. It is a pity that they were not able to invest in the cottages themselves for then Wycoller might have benefitted from the immense rise in the property values rather than suffer from the exploitation that was to occur.

What of the Water Board, the Colne Borough Council and the Trawden Urban District Council? They do not come out of the story with much honour. It is unfortunate that matters of history and culture should have ever become dependent on the cold decision of a Water Board. Those who continued the struggle for

Wycoller were people with the ability to understand the quality of living, to see that life is not simply the building of a machine, the efficient production of water or the construction of a reservoir. They were people from all walks of life and they worked so that those of like spirit could take pleasure after them.

Country Park

A public meeting

In October 1972 a public meeting was held in Colne to discuss the question of making a Country Park at Wycoller. The Lancashire County Council was considering buying and developing land at Wycoller for a Country Park under the Town and Country Planning Act of 1967. Plans were displayed showing the boundaries of the proposed Conservation Area and Country Park and ways in which it might be developed. The meeting was held not only to discuss the situation but also to ask for observations to be submitted to County Hall.

To those who had been Friends of Wycoller it seemed unbelievable that what they had struggled for so long to achieve was now apparently being offered to them on a plate. Buildings were to be restored and those in the village protected as in a Conservation Area, the Hall ruins were to be made safe and preserved from further deterioration, cars were to be kept out of the centre, a warden was to be in charge, picnic areas were to be provided, and much more besides.

The meeting was a lively one as Colne was still not short of characters. Members of the old Colne Borough Council sitting on the front row bickered with each other and caused interruptions. A further councillor took the stage and harangued the meeting with irrelevancies until he was persuaded to sit down. Above all else strong animosity was expressed towards the Water Board from many sources. Alderman Stephen Shaw, Chairman of the North Calder Water Board, addressed the meeting with dignity, saying that he was obviously cast as the villain of the piece. He explained that he had felt a responsibility towards Wycoller but often it was a responsibility that he was inadequate to meet. However, he was able to report that the Water Board was unanimously in favour of the proposed Country Park project. That evening there were questions from farmers, ramblers, councillors and local historians, and the verdict seemed unanimous—Wycoller should be preserved as a Country Park.

Of course, there was a reason for the county's involvement with Wycoller; it had not just suddenly occurred to someone in County

Hall that here was a worthwhile project. To follow this development we must go back to around 1966 when the influence of the societies which had protected Wycoller was waining. Slowly the threat of exploitation grew. Cottages which had been sold around 1965 for as little as £150 began to change hands at high prices. This rise in prices was of no benefit to Wycoller: it was money being exploited not invested in the village. Wycoller was, as always, a popular subject for the press, and countless articles appeared discussing the question of development, accompanied by the usual mixture of bogus history and legend.

On 15 March 1972 the *Evening Star* announced the sale of the Wycoller Estate for £11,000. Colin Simmonds, Town Clerk of Nelson and Clerk to the North Calder Water Board, was quoted as saying: "The terms were agreed before Christmas and the preparations of documents, plans and boundaries has been going on since then". The buyer was reported to be Albert Wilkinson of Lowlands Farm. There is no doubt that the publicity given by the *Evening Star* on that occasion set off a series of events leading to the plans for a Country Park by the end of the year. Although the terms of sale were said to have been agreed it was obvious that the sale had not been completed and in view of this James Preston, former owner of Lyons Tours in Colne, made an offer of £15,000.

The *Evening Star* followed developments closely and on 7 April an article appeared headed: "What is going on in Wycoller?" This reported the story about the purchase and the comments of the Clerk to the Water Board but added the information about the £15,000 offer by James Preston. Further enquiries had met with a wall of silence. Colin Simmonds, Clerk to the Water Board was "unavailable for comment" and the would-be-buyer would only comment: "There has been too much publicity about it already I have absolutely nothing to say". A spokesman for Dacre Son and Hartley, estate agents of Skipton who had been handling negotiations for the buyer, had also nothing to say. James Preston had nothing to say. However, at the Department of the Environment in London a spokesman confirmed that an offer of £15,000 had been received for the village of Wycoller alone and that the earlier deal was off.

Those concerned about Wycoller's future were disturbed to hear that surveys had been made in the village with a view to the private development of property there. About this time a bulldozer arrived

Photographer Arthur Charlesworth captioned this
ominous picture "Waiting in the Wings"

in Wycoller to demolish property opposite Wycoller House. The demolition aroused anger. Surely no individual should have the right to demolish any part of Wycoller's heritage irrespective of ownership. The cottage was demolished and the vehicle of destruction sat ominously on the village green.

A report to the Society for the Preservation of Ancient Buildings reported that: "Even if sympathetic owners are found for the houses a serious problem would remain in the maintenance of the setting— the bridges, barns, outbuildings, the river, road, and trees . . . Some scheme of communal ownership of the setting with the local authority is necessary to preserve it as a whole. Although the ruin is listed, we feel that the Department of the Environment should be urged to list the village in its entirety". After much activity behind the scenes, speculation and rumour came to an end in September 1972 with the announcement of the Wycoller Park scheme.

198

In 1973 the Lancashire County Council Planning Department issued a booklet *Wycoller Country Park and Conservation Area* which outlined details of the proposed work at Wycoller. The historical background was fortunately brief, being comprised of a handful of mixed errors and half-truths. However, the main body of the booklet listed scores of encouraging plans for the restoration of the village. The conservation policy is, according to the booklet, "in order that Wycoller may be rehabilitated and restored to its original condition", sounding as though Wycoller were a piece of Georgian furniture awaiting restoration. It must, however, be remembered that Wycoller has been changing through the centuries and therefore has no 'original condition'. Even with the restoration of all existing buildings, since some thirty dwellings have disappeared modern Wycoller will still only be a fragment of the Victorian village.

Fate has preserved Wycoller and its beautiful Dene from the horrors of the Industrial Revolution, preserved it from motor roads, and preserved it, when it seemed doomed to certain flood. Let us hope that Wycoller will now be allowed to move gracefully through a few more centuries.

Sources and Notes

INTRODUCTION
1. In 1973, during the preparation of this book a photographic booklet entitled *Wycoller* by S. Cookson and H. Hindle was published by Hendon Publishing Co. Ltd. In 1974 it was revised and reprinted under the title *Wycoller Country Park*.

CHAPTER 1: ARROW-HEADS AND AXES
1. Hammer stone: *Cartwright Museum Archaeological Group Bulletin* Vol. 3, No. 3, March 1958.
2. Saddle quern: *Cartwright Museum Archaeological Group Bulletin* Vol. 2, No. 11, November 1957. Quern removed to Scotland by finder Joe Davies.
3. Flint workshop: *Colne and Nelson Times*, 17 November 1899.

CHAPTER 2: VACCARIES IN THE FOREST.
1. The landowners of Trawden Forest: *The Royal Forest of Lancashire*, R. C. Shaw, c.15.
2. The Rev. T. D. Whitaker *The History of Whalley*, 1st Ed. 1801 p.170.
3. Further explanation of forest: Rev. T. D. Whitaker, as above p.160. "implied a tract of land lying out (foras) that is rejected, as of no value".
4. *De Lacy Compoti A.D.* 1296–1305, Lyons P.A., p.157.
5. W. Bennett, *History of Marsden and Nelson*, p.17.
6. Trawden Forest raids and other information W. Farrer, *Clitheroe Court Rolls*.

CHAPTER 3: TUDOR TIMES.
1. In the Decree of 1507 and Hartley land disputes of 1537 abbreviations have been extended but the original spelling has been retained.
2. Quotations from Wills and Inventories: Probate Records Diocese of Chester 1487–1858, Lancashire Record Office.

3. Will of William Hargreaves: Probate Records Diocese of York, Borthwick Institute of Historical Research, St. Anthony's Hall, York. Probate Register 27, f 338 & 339.
4. Quotation William Harrison: G. M. Trevelyan, *English Social History*, p.129.

CHAPTER 4: STUART PERIOD.
1. Copyholders 1608: J. Carr, *Annals and Stories of Colne and Neighbourhood*, p.222.
2. Marriages of John Cunliffe: *Romantic Wycoller* and Cunliffe pedigrees. Memorial in Altham Church says John Cunliffe was born 1 November 1614 thus being only 14 years when he is said to have married Grace Hartley in 1628. There were possibly two John Cunliffes of the same generation.
3. The account of Civil War in Lancashire is based on the account given by W. Bennett in *The History of Marsden and Nelson*, pp.106–110.
4. Poll Tax Wycoller 1660: photostat copies Colne Library. Ref. E 179/250/4 roll 41, 84–85, Public Record Office, London.
5. Sufferings books 1653–1720, Society of Friends' Records, FRM/1/39 1660–1694, Lancashire Record Office.
6. Surrender of land by John Kippax: Susanah Benson documents. Susanah Benson was the daughter of Richard Hartley of Wycoller. She inherited estates in 1892, married Watson Benson in 1896 and died in 1911. On the death of Watson Benson in 1943 the Wycoller property passed back to the Hartley family in the person of H. R. Hartley of Bridge End Farm, Rimington. Although the family no longer own any property in Wycoller over a thousand deeds and documents relating to Wycoller had been stored under a bed at the farm. In 1973 the documents were deposited at the Lancashire Record Office by Richard Hartley, H. R. Hartley's son. Ref. DDX/905.

CHAPTER 5: THOMAS EYRE'S ACCOUNT.
1. Main information concerning Thomas Eyre: *Lancashire and Cheshire Antiquarian Society Notes*, Vol. 2, 1885–1886, pp.105–112. The article by W. A. Abram was based on a MS in the Chetham Library at Manchester. Original MS reported misplaced 1974.
2. Supercargo — person in merchantship managing sales of cargo.
3. Will of Henry Cunliffe, 1769, proved 1773. Probate Records Diocese of York, Borthwick Institute, York.

CHAPTER 6: THE LAST SQUIRE.
1. The unpublished diaries of Elizabeth Shackleton are deposited in the Lancashire Record Office Ref. DDB/8. The extracts relating to Henry Owen Cunliffe have not previously appeared in print.

CHAPTER 7: GHOSTS AND LEGENDS.
1. The Lad of Crow Hill: DDBd/41/15 Wycoller Boundaries, Lancashire Record Office.
2. J. Harland and T. T. Wilkinson, *Lancashire Legends*, p.79.
3. Fred Bannister, *The Annals of Trawden Forest*, p.79.

CHAPTER 8: WYCOLLER IN LITERATURE.
1. The Spectre Horseman by Frank Slater original publication of 1918, printed in pamphlet form by F. Wormwell, Colne, Loaned by S. Cookson, Trawden.
2. Charlotte Brontë, *Jayne Eyre*, C.37.
3. *Lancashire and Cheshire Antiquarian Society Transactions*, 1901, vol. 19, p.251.
4. Halliwell Sutcliffe publications approx., 1895–1935.

CHAPTER 9: PEOPLE AND WORK.
1. Earliest surnames from vaccary references, Tudor names from probate records and parish registers.
2. The account of Benjamin Ingham's entry into Lancashire: William Batty's manuscript Church History deposited in the Methodist Archives and Research Centre, London. Microfilm copy Colne Library.
3. William Darney's rhyme from *Methodist Heroes in the Great Haworth Round*, 1734–1784, Laycock. J. W., Keighley, 1909.
4. Worsted weaving statistics: W. Bennett, *History of Marsden and Nelson*, p.129.
5. Population figures and occupations: Census Returns of 1841, 1851, 1861, 1871. Microfilm copies Colne Library, from originals at the P.R.O., London.
6. 'Delaine' probably Mousseline de Laine a lightweight woollen cloth of plain weave.
7. Timmy Feather's handloom and weaving equipment at Cliffe Castle Museum, Keighley. Photographs by courtesy of the Cliffe Castle Museum.

CHAPTER 10: FARMS, FIELDS AND COTTAGES.
1. Height Laithe termed "Wuthering Heights": Lancashire and Cheshire Antiquarian Society Transactions 1901, vol. 19., p.251.
2. Foster Leap deeds DDX/905 Lancashire Record Office.
3. Herders: *Colne and Nelson Times*, 6 July, 1923.
4. Two headed calf: *Colne Times*, 25 May and 1 June 1923.
5. Trawden Tithe Award 1844, DRB/1/188 and Trawden Enclosure Award 1821, Lancashire Record Office.

CHAPTER 11: VALLEY OF THE SEVEN BRIDGES.
1. The Ministry of Works report on pack-horse bridge included in report on Wycoller Hall dated 15 November 1948. Files of Friends of Wycoller, Colne Library.
2. Wycoller bridges: Rev. C. S. Sargisson, *A Lancashire Moorland Oasis, The Graphic*, 18 March 1911.
3. Timber bridge: *Colne Times*, 1 and 22 July 1966.

CHAPTER 12: SAVED FROM THE FLOOD.
1. The Colne Corporation Act 1897, 60 & 61 Vic. 2/2639 clxxxi.
2. Wycoller reservoir plans loaned by W. M. Spencer, F.L.A.
3. Wycoller Bore Hole, article on geology by Dr A. Wilmore, F.G.S., *Colne Times*, 4 October 1901.
4. The Water Department's Annual Reports, 1928 to 1959: Colne Library.

CHAPTER 13: FRIENDS AND PRESERVATION.
1. Friends of Wycoller files: Colne Library. Treasurer's files loaned by W. M. Spencer, F.L.A., Colne.
2. Wycoller Preservation Committee correspondence loaned by Douglas Barber, B.A., Nelson and Colne College of Further Education.

CHAPTER 14: COUNTRY PARK.
1. Report on Wycoller for the Society for the Preservation of Ancient Buildings by Nikolas Astley and David Jeffcoate, 31 December 1971. Report based on a visit of 27 October 1971.

Bibliography

Bannister, F.	*The Annals of Trawden Forest*, Colne & Nelson Times,	1922
Bennett, W.	*The History of Marsden and Nelson*, Nelson Corporation,	1957
Bennett, W.	*The History of Burnley*, vol. 1., Burnley Corporation,	1946
Carr, J.	*Annals and Stories of Colne and Neighbourhood*,	1878
Eckwall, E.	*Place Names of Lancashire*, Chetham Society, vol. 81.,	1922
Emmott, T.C.	*An Outlaw in the Twentieth Century*, Emmotts Wycoller,	1964
Emmott, T.C.	*Eamot Eternal*, Emmotts Wycoller,	1952
Farrer, W.	*Court Rolls of the Honor of Clitheroe*, vol. 1., Manchester,	1897
Folley, E.W.	*Romantic Wycoller*, Privately Published,	1949
Gaskell, E.C.	*The Life of Charlotte Brontë*, Smith & Elder,	1857
Gregson, M.	*Portfolio of Fragments - Lancashire*, Routledge, 3rd. ed.,	1869
Harland, J. & Wilkinson, T.T.	*Lancashire Legends*, Heywood,	1882
Lyons, P.A.	*De Lacy Compoti. A.D. 1296–1305*, Chetham Society,	1884
Newbigging, T.	*History of the Forest of Rossendale*,	1893
Ordnance Survey,	*Field Archaeology, Some Notes for Beginners*, Professional Papers, New Series, no. 13., H.M.S.O.	1963
Owen, Major General C.H.	*The Descendants of the Elder Branch of the Cunliffes of Wycoller*, Spottiswood & Co.,	1871
Shaw, Dr. R.C.	*The Royal Forest of Lancashire*, Preston,	1956
Stenton, D.M.	*English Society in the Early Middle Ages*, Penguin,	1951
Trevelyan, G.M.	*English Social History*, Longmans, 3rd. Imp.,	1945
Whitaker, Rev. T.D.	*History of Whalley*, Blackburn,	1801
Wood, N.	*Visions and Voices*, Privately Pub.,	No Date
Wroot, H.F.	*The Persons and Places of Brontë Novels*, Brontë Society,	1906

Index

References in **bold type** refer to illustrations.

Alkincoats Hall, 73, 74, 76, 84, 85, 88.
An Outlaw in the Twentieth Century, 115.
Austen, Jane, 76, 77.
Aylward, Maureen, 192.
Ambler,
  Alice, 55.
  Anne, 55.
  Elizabeth, 55, 60.
  James, 55, 60.
  John, 55, 60.
  Marie, 55.
  Mary, 60.
  Thomas, 55.
Atkinson, James, 54.

Bainbridge, T.M., 147.
Bank House, 146, 178, 180.
Bannister,
  Fred, 88, 93, 97, 153, 202.
  John, 51, 53.
Barber, Douglas, 191, 192, 203.
Barnsley, 63, 64, 65.
Batty, William, 131, 202.
Beardshaw, 21, 23, 33.
Bennett, Walter, 17, 54.
Benson,
  Susanah, 177, 180, 201.
  Watson, 183, 201.
Bernard, Daniel, 51.
Black Bess, ghost, 91, 93.
Blackburn, 52, 54.
Bobbin Mill, 159.
Bolling Hall, 33, 34.
Bolton Abbey School, 73.
Bore Hole, 180, 181, 182, 203.
Boroughbridge, Battle of, 26.
Bosworth Field, Battle of, 30.
Boulsworth Hill, 10, 13, 21, 81, 88, 98, **99**, 161, 181.
Boyd-Dawkins, Professor, 180.
Bracewell,
  Kenneth 95.
  William, 95, 96, 150, 183.
Bracken Hills, 147.
Bradford, 81.
Brigantes, 16, 17.
Brink Ends, 15, 181.
Brontë,
  Charlotte, 81, 89, 122, **122**, 124, 125, 126, 127, 202.
  Emily, 125.
  Family 122, 187.
Brontë Society, 125, 185, 188.
Bronze Age, 12, 13, 15, 16, 25.
Browsholme, 74.
Bruce, Robert, 25.
Burnley, 26, 54, 109, 115, 126, 133.

Carr Hall, 74, 76.
Charles I, 51.

Charles II, 20, 91, 100.
Chetham,
  Mary, 50 51.
  Ralph, 51.
Civil War, 51.
Clam Bridge, 16, 24, 173, **174**.
Clapper Bridge, 171, 172, **172**.
Clayton, Thomas, 74, 75, 84, 86, 88.
Clegg, James, 54.
Clitheroe, 52, 54.
  Castle, 32, 161.
  Honor of, 20, 21, 22, 28, 49.
Cockfighting, 80, 81, 128.
Cock Pit, **83**.
Colne, 32, 36, 51, 52, 53, 65, 71, 74, 76, 83, 109, 131, 133, 138, 177, 178, 185, 196.
  Cloth Hall, 132, **132**, 179.
  Corporation, 177, 180, 182, 183, 185, 186, 187, 203.
  Cross, 84.
  Operatic Society, 110, 188.
  Parish Church, 50, 58, 65, 66, 70, 80, 86, 100, 130.
  Town Hall, 179, 185.
  Water Department, 182, 183, 184, 192, 203.
Combe Hill, 11, 12, 15, 21, 25, 181.
Combe Hill Cross, 143, **143**.
Combes House, 143, 145.
Cookson, Stanley, 15, 200, 202.
Copy House, 146, **146**, 173, 178, 180.
Country Park, 11, 196, 197, 198.
Cunliffe,
  Anne, 51, 63, 64, 67, 69.
  Baron, 73, 80, 81.
  Elizabeth, 50, 51, 54, 56, 63, 64, 71, 126.
  Ellis, 50, 51, 54, 56, 100.
  Foster, 65, 100.
  Henry, 62-68, 71, 73, 100, 201.
  Henry Owen, 50, 61, 64, 65, 72, 73, 74, 76, 77, 80, 81, 83, 84, 86, 87, 98, 132, 141, 143, 151, 152, 171.
  Isabel, 54.
  Jane, 51.
  Joan, 66.
  John, 50, 51, 54, 63, 64, 75, 153, 201.
  Kathleen, 51.
  Margaret, 51.
  Mary, 51, 69, 71, 86, 87.
  Nicholas, 50, 51, 52, 54, 55, 56, 63, 64, 65.
  Robert, 50, 51, 52, 54.
  Simon, 91, 127.
  Squire, 82.
  Thomasin, 55, 56.
  William, 63-66.

Darney, William, 131, 202.
Davies, Joe, 11, 12, 200.
Dean House, 146, 178, 180.
Dene Cottage, 119, 148, 191.
(see Thistleholme Cottage)

205

Dewhurst,
  Frank, 93, 94, 158.
  Judith 94, **103**.
  Nesta, 93, 94, **103**, 158.
Dialogus, 19.
Disafforestation, 31, 32.
Driver, Geoffrey, 34, 46.
Druid's Bridge, 173 (see Clapper Bridge)

Eamot Eternal, 115, 121, **121**.
Edward II, 20, 26.
Emmott,
  Elizabeth, 38-41, 44, 45, 49.
  Ellen, 38, 44.
  Family, 81, 130.
  George, 59.
  Henry de, 21.
  James, 59.
  John, 49.
  Richard, 34.
  Robert, 38, 49, 55, 59.
  Thomas, 28, 46.
  Thomas Clifford, 115-121, **118**, 168, 188.
  William, 28, 41, 46.
Emmott's Cottage, 115, **116**, 150, 158.
  (see Wycoller Cottage)
Eyre,
  Catherine, 64, 71.
  Elizabeth (Betty), 64, 67, 70, 126.
  Family, 60, 61, 126.
  Mary, 64.
  Thomas, 63-71, 126.

Fairbank,
  Elizabeth, 60.
  John, 60.
  Maria, 60.
  Michael, 60, 61.
Far Cross Farm, 143.
Farrer, William, 32.
Feather,
  Maria, 141.
  Timmy, 135, **136**, 202.
  Thomas, 141.
Ferndean Manor, 122-127, 185.
Field Names, 160, 161, 164, 165.
Folley, E.W., 29, 99, 102, 124, **124**, 125, 148, 152, 159, 189, 191.
Foster Leap Farm, 100, 139, **140**, 203.
  Rocks, 100, **111**.
Foulds,
  Alderman Robinson, 180.
  Anne, 55, 59, 60.
  Catherine, 33.
  Councillor E.A., 182.
  Geoffrey, 33, 34.
  James, 33, 55, 58, 59.
  John, 33, 37, 49, 55, 146.
  Mark, 142.
  Peter, 34.
  Richard, 132.
Friends of Wycoller, 153, 184, 186-191, 194, 196.

Gaskell, Mrs. E.C., 81, 82, 89, 126.
Gawthorpe Hall, 52, 126, 127.
Green, Charles, 11, 190.

Guytrash Padfoot, 88, 89, 90, 127.

Hall Bridge, (see Clapper Bridge)
Hammer Stone, 10, **11**
Hammond, John, 51.
Hanson, John, 33.
Hargreaves,
  James, 54.
  William, 42, 44, 132.
Harrison, William, 45, 46, 201.
Hartley,
  Alison, 54, 58.
  Barnard, 34, 54, 58.
  Cecily, 33.
  Christopher, 33, 34, 35, 46, 54, 58.
  Elizabeth, 50, 54, 55, 58.
  Geoffrey, 27, 33, 34, 44, 46.
  Gilbert, 33.
  Grace, 50, 201.
  Helen, 54.
  Henry, 28, 46.
  Herbert Richard, 185-187, 201.
  Isabel, 58.
  James, 34, 37, 46, 49, 54, 58, 59, 87.
  John, 28, 33-37, 42, 46, 49, 58.
  John alias Byrdye, 46.
  John alias Hoydye, 46.
  John alias Pyenose, 46.
  Margaret, 58.
  Nicholas, 33.
  Peter, 33-36, 46, 49, 151.
  Piers, 149, 151.
  Richard, 33, 87, 143, 157, 177, 201.
  Robert, 27, 28, 46.
  Roger, 33-39, 42, 44, 45, 46, 49, 54, 55, 58, 161.
  Roger alias Little Hog, 33, 34, 46.
  Roger alias Pynnes, 46.
  Sarah, 55.
  Susanah, 157.
  William, 46.
Hawk House (see Oak House).
Haworth, 13, 81, 97, 117, 125, 127, 131, 185.
Haworth, David, 159.
Heathcoat, Sarah, 64, 71.
Height Laithe Farm, 24, 43, 60, 61, 89, 134, **139**, 178, 203.
Henry VII, 30.
Herders Inn, 111, 127, 128, **141**, 142, 203.
Hill, William, 85.
Hindle,
  Elizabeth, 138.
  Hartley, 138.
  Henry, 138.
  Herbert, 200.
Hoghton, Sir Gilbert, 51.
Hollins, 54, 63, 64, 65.

Ightenhill, 25, 26.
Ingham, Benjamin, 130, 131, 202.
Iron Age, 12, 16.
Isabella, 20, 26.

James I, 48.
Jane Eyre, 89, 122, 124, 125, 127, 185, 202.
Jowett, Evelyn, 85, 188.

206

Kay-Shuttleworth,
　Sir James, 126.
　Lady Janet, 126.
Key Stiles Farm, 139, 142, **142**.
Kippax,
　Alison, 55, 58, 146
　Edward, 56.
　John, 55, 56, 58, 146, 201.
　William, 56, 58.
Kippax Tenement, 58, 146.

Lacy de,
　Accounts, 21, 22.
　Alice, 19.
　Henry, 19, 20.
　Ilbert, 19.
Lad Law, 98, **99**.
Lad of Crow Hill, 97, **97**, 98.
Laithe Hills Barn, 156, **157**, 183.
Laithe Hills Bridge, 168, **169**.
Laithe Hills Cottage, 155, **156**, 191, 193.
Laithe Hills Cottages, 156, **169**.
Lancashire and Cheshire Antiquarian Society, 126, 201.
Lancaster, 51, 52.
　Sheriff of, 20.
　Thomas Earl of, 20, 25, 26.
Lancastrian Party, 118.
Lant Trough, **44**.
Leeds, 63, 64, 66.
Liverpool, 65, 100.
London, 77, 132, 197.
Lonesome Heights, 127.
Lowcock, William, 58, 146.
Lowlands Bridge, 167, **167**, 168, 190.
Lowlands Farm, 95, 148, 167, 197.
Lund, John, 141.

Makin, William, 100.
Manchester, 77, 84.
Manwood, John, 141.
Map, Ordnance Survey,
　Township, 162, 163.
　Village 1893, 154.
Marsden Hall, 74-76.
Mellelieu, Jim, 190.
Mesolithic, 9, 17.
Midgely, Dr., 84.
Militia,
　Craven, 83.
　Lancashire, 83.
Ministry of Works, 170, 171, 187, 190, 203.
Monck, General George, 20.
Morville,
　Anne, 64.
　Walter, 65.
Murrain, 23.

Near Cross Farm, 143, 145.
Neolithic, 10, 12, 13, 17.
North Calder Water Board, 155, 159, 176, 192, 193, 194, 196, 197.
Nussey, Ellen, 125.

Oak House, 147, 180, 194.
Oddie, Matthew, 85, 86.

Old Hall Cottage, 179, 183, 184, **184**.
Oldham,
　Adam, 76.
　Hannah, 77, 87.
　John, 87.
　Mary, 64, 77.
　Rev. John Roberts, 87.
Oldham Arms, (see Herders Inn)
Owen,
　Charles Cunliffe, 64, 86.
　Henry, 64, 72, 73.
　Joseph, 63, 64, 67, 73.
　Major General C.H., 171.
　Sarah (Sally) 171.

Pack-Horse Bridge, 170, **170**, **172**.
Parker,
　Family, 84, 85.
　John, 73, 74, 80, 81, 88.
　Robert (Robin) 74.
　Thomas (Tom) 73, 74, 80, 83, 86, 88.
Parson Lee Farm, 11, 86, 89, 139, 145. **145**, 146, 174, 178.
　Out Laithe, 11.
Pasture House, 74, 75, 86.
Pearson,
　Henry, 149.
　John, 61, 62, 152.
Pearson's Farm, 87, 95, **96**, 148, 149, **149**, 168, 180, 190.
Pendle Hill, 73, 181.
Pepper Hill Cottages, 156.
Pickersgill, Joan, 64, 66.
Pickles,
　Grace, 55.
　Michael, 55.
Poll Tax 1660, 54-56, 58-60.
Population, 130, 137, 138.
Pott, Lanslett John, R.A., 82.
Preston,
　Family, 146.
　James, 197.
　Thomas, 146.
　William, 146.
Preston, 51, 52, 80, 159.
Pygmy Flints, 9.

Quakers, 56-58, 130.

Raven Rock Farm, 139, 147.
Red Lion, 74, 76, 80.
Ricroft of Withens, 141.
Riley,
　Family, 140.
　Janet, 55, 60.
　Robert, 55, 60.
　Richard, 134.
　Susan, 55.
　Susanah, 61.
　William, 134.
Robert, Lawrence, 46.
Rochester, Mr., 89, 122, 127.
Roger Laithe, (see Combes House)
Romantic Wycoller, 29, 99, 124, 148, 151, 153, 159, 171.
Rossendale, Forest of, 20, 21, 26, 52.

207

Royal Forest, 18, 19.

Saddle Quern, 11, 12.
Sagar, John, 56.
Sargisson, Rev. C.S., 172, 203.
Scargill,
  John, 63, 64.
  Sarah (Sally) 63, 64, 65, 171.
Shackleton,
  Alderman J.W., 185.
  Elizabeth, 74, 75, 80, 83, 84, 86, 88, 201, 202.
  Family, 73, 86.
  John, 33, 74, 76, 77.
  Percy, 152.
  Richard, 46.
Shaw,
  Alderman Stephen, 196.
  Anne, 55.
  Jack, 84.
  John, 55.
  Thomasin, 55.
Sheffield, 63, 65, 69, 71-73, 76.
Shirley, 125.
Shuttleworth, Richard, 51.
Skipton, 26, 52, 54.
  Castle, 26, 67.
Slater, Frank, 91, 109, 111, **111**, 188, 202.
Smith,
  Fred, 158.
  Isabel, 60.
  Margaret, 55, 60.
  Richard, 55.
  Robert, 58, 60.
  William, 60.
Smithy Clough, 141, 144, **144**, 145.
Society for the Preservation of Ancient Buildings, 185, 187, 198.
Spectre Horseman, 88, 90, **90**, 91, 93, 111-115, 202.
Stansfield, Harry, 14.
Sunderland, Joseph, 147.
Sutcliffe, Halliwell, 89, 91, 127, 129, 141, 202.

Tempest, Sir Richard, 33, 34.
Thistleholme,
  Cottage, 148, **148**, 192, (see Dene Cottage)
  Farm, 148.
Thornfield Hall, 125.
Through Sorrow's Gates, 127, 128, 141.
Topham,
  Anne, 68, 71.
  Lupton, 67, 69.
  Mary, 64, 67.
Towneley Hall, 68, 74.
Trawden Enclosure Act, 161.

Trawden Tithe Award, 142, 160, 161, 164, 165, 203.
Two-headed calf, 147, **147**.

Unlawful Games, 37.

Vaccary Walls, 23, 24, **24**.
Varley,
  Hannah, 157.
  John, 157.
  William, 157.

Wallbank,
  Family, 140.
  John, 144.
  Susan, 144.
  William, 144.
Walton, Family, 74, 81, 86.
Water Board (see North Calder Water Board)
Watson, Matthew, 180.
Weaver's Bridge 172 (see Clapper Bridge)
Weaving, 39, 43, 131-138.
Webster,
  Elizabeth, (Betty) 64, 66, 67.
  John, 64, 66, 67.
Wesley, John, 131.
Whalley, Peter, 13, 14.
Whitaker, John, 60, 132.
Wightman, Peter, 99.
Wilkinson,
  Alfred, 95, 197.
  Edmund, 149.
  Shirley, 94.
Wilmore, A. F.G.S., 181.
Wimperis, Edmund Morison, 125.
Wood,
  Dorothy, 64.
  Nesta, 102, **103**.
Wroot, H.F., 125.
Wuzzin, 39, **42**, **43**.
Wycoller,
  Cottage, 115, **116**, 150, 158, 193.
  Farm, 95, 148, 150, 158.
  House, 93, 94, **94**, **103**, 157-159, 169, 198.
  Preservation Committee, 155, 191-194.
  Reservoir Scheme, 177-180, 186.
Wycoller Hall, 61, **61**, 62, 64, 65, **66**, 67-69, 73, 74, 76, 77, **79**, 80, 82-84, 86, **87**, 88-93, **92**, 95, 100, 101, **105**, **106**, 110, 122, 124-128, 141, 149, 150, **150**, 151-153, 159, 167, 178, 182, 184-190, 194.
  Barn, 153, **155**, 159.
  Farm, 180, 183.
  Porch, 77, **78**, 153.
  Renovations, 77.
Wyld, Lydia, 187, 188, 191.